ACTION MATHS

4th CLASS

FOLENS

Introduction to teachers and parents

Action Maths has been developed by a team of experienced primary teachers and consultants in accordance with the aims and objectives of the revised Primary Maths Curriculum and the accompanying Teacher Guidelines.

The series underpins the key areas of:

- use of concrete materials
- development and correct use of

- mathematical language
- real-life problem solving
- cooperative group work
- oral maths

- estimation
- written computation
- integration with other subjects

Action Maths is a creative new maths series that aims to equip children for the 21st century.

Consultants

Valerie O'Dowd, Ena Fitzpatrick

Authors

Clifford Brown (6th), Denis Courtney (5th), Liam Gaynor (3rd & 4th),
Trina Cooney (3rd), Thérèse Dooley (2nd), Francis Connolly (1st), Yvonne Keating (1st),
Angela Curley (Senior Infants), Jacqueline O'Donohoe (Senior Infants),
Deirdre Whelan (Junior Infants)

Editor: Aoife Barrett
Book & Cover Design: Philip Ryan
Layout: Design Image
Illustration: Brian Fitzgerald, Monica Kennedy, John Leonard,
Graham-Cameron Illustration: Tony O'Donnell, Mandy Lillywhite, Claire Boyce,
Natalie Bould, Rodney Sutton, Felicity House, Nicola Sedgwick

ISBN 0 86121 959 7

© Folens Publishers 2002
First published in 2002 by Folens Publishers,
Hibernian Industrial Estate, Greenhills Road, Tallaght, Dublin 24.
Printed at the press of the publisher

Contents

ROBERT THE BRUCE

One evening after his army had been beaten in a terrible battle, King Robert the Bruce lay in a cave. He was in a very bad mood and felt like giving everything up. In his anger, he smashed a lovely web that a little spider had just made. To his amazement the spider just made another web – even better than the last! Robert smiled to himself as he realised that you should never give up. You should try and try and you will succeed.

If you sometimes feel that maths is a bit hard and you feel like giving up, just remember this story about Robert the Bruce.

1. a.　8 + 5 = ☐　　b.　9 + 4 = ☐　　c.　10 + 7 = ☐

　 d.　17 + 6 = ☐　　e.　12 + 3 = ☐　　f.　13 + 6 = ☐

　 g.　14 + 7 = ☐　　h.　21 + 8 = ☐　　i.　19 + 2 = ☐

2. a.　10 − 3 = ☐　　b.　13 − 4 = ☐　　c.　15 − 8 = ☐

　 d.　21 − 7 = ☐　　e.　25 − 6 = ☐　　f.　30 − 3 = ☐

　 g.　31 − 6 = ☐　　h.　44 − 5 = ☐　　i.　18 − 9 = ☐

3. a.　(8 + 5) − 6 = ☐　　b.　(10 + 6) − 5 = ☐　　c.　(9 + 9) − 2 = ☐

　 d.　(7 + 11) − 5 = ☐　　e.　(12 + 4) − 3 = ☐　　f.　(14 + 7) − 6 = ☐

　 g.　(15 + 12) − 9 = ☐　　h.　(9 + 13) − 12 = ☐　　i.　(11 + 9) − 4 = ☐

4. **Make up a question for each answer.**

　 a.　12　　　　　b.　28c　　　　c.　35 animals

　 d.　24 days　　　e.　50 people　　f.　5 hours

　 g.　3 apples each　h.　30 sweets　　i.　€240

　 j.　80 pages　　　k.　12 pens　　　l.　5 each and 1 left over

1. a.
$$\begin{array}{r} 23 \\ + 45 \\ \hline \end{array}$$
   b.
$$\begin{array}{r} 35 \\ + 35 \\ \hline \end{array}$$
   c.
$$\begin{array}{r} 46 \\ + 74 \\ \hline \end{array}$$
   d.
$$\begin{array}{r} 35 \\ + 57 \\ \hline \end{array}$$
   e.
$$\begin{array}{r} 37 \\ + 28 \\ \hline \end{array}$$
   f.
$$\begin{array}{r} 57 \\ + 79 \\ \hline \end{array}$$

2. a.
$$\begin{array}{r} 244 \\ + 184 \\ \hline \end{array}$$
   b.
$$\begin{array}{r} 462 \\ + 382 \\ \hline \end{array}$$
   c.
$$\begin{array}{r} 263 \\ + 109 \\ \hline \end{array}$$
   d.
$$\begin{array}{r} 183 \\ + 291 \\ \hline \end{array}$$
   e.
$$\begin{array}{r} 270 \\ + 37 \\ \hline \end{array}$$
   f.
$$\begin{array}{r} 106 \\ + 519 \\ \hline \end{array}$$

3. a.
$$\begin{array}{r} 84 \\ - 23 \\ \hline \end{array}$$
   b.
$$\begin{array}{r} 56 \\ - 45 \\ \hline \end{array}$$
   c.
$$\begin{array}{r} 28 \\ - 17 \\ \hline \end{array}$$
   d.
$$\begin{array}{r} 78 \\ - 39 \\ \hline \end{array}$$
   e.
$$\begin{array}{r} 73 \\ - 45 \\ \hline \end{array}$$
   f.
$$\begin{array}{r} 97 \\ - 28 \\ \hline \end{array}$$

4. a.
$$\begin{array}{r} 424 \\ - 404 \\ \hline \end{array}$$
   b.
$$\begin{array}{r} 632 \\ - 599 \\ \hline \end{array}$$
   c.
$$\begin{array}{r} 300 \\ - 137 \\ \hline \end{array}$$
   d.
$$\begin{array}{r} 400 \\ - 273 \\ \hline \end{array}$$
   e.
$$\begin{array}{r} 999 \\ - 678 \\ \hline \end{array}$$
   f.
$$\begin{array}{r} 231 \\ - 109 \\ \hline \end{array}$$

5. a. $9 + 56 + 123 =$ ☐   b. $45 + 229 + 118 =$ ☐

   c. $331 + 558 + 9 =$ ☐   d. $158 + 55 + 227 =$ ☐

   e. $449 + 82 + 371 =$ ☐   f. $552 + 23 + 168 =$ ☐

   g. $892 - 228 =$ ☐   h. $558 - 227 =$ ☐

   i. $917 - 229 =$ ☐   j. $900 - 258 =$ ☐

   k. $230 - 178 =$ ☐   l. $450 - 369 =$ ☐

6. **Double each of these numbers:**
   a. 7   b. 11   c. 13   d. 21   e. 25   f. 31

   g. 33   h. 40   i. 51   j. 60   k. 18   l. 36

7. Sheila collected 115 football cards and Mark collected 91 football cards.
   How many cards did they collect altogether?

8. A large restaurant has seating for 128 people.
   76 of the seats are occupied.
   How many seats are not occupied?

9. A history book with a total of 440 pages is divided
   into 2 parts. The first part has 198 pages.
   How many pages are there in the second part?

10. A woman won €800. She spent €370 of it on a holiday
    and €248 on a new video. How much money has she left?

1. a. 23   b. 24   c. 17   d. 19   e. 41   f. 32
    x 2   x 3   x 5   x 7   x 9   x 6

2. a. 75   b. 83   c. 18   d. 64   e. 62   f. 77
    x 5   x 6   x 5   x 9   x 6   x 8

3. **Multiply each of these numbers by 10. Example: 34 x 10 = 340.**
    a. 36   b. 56   c. 87   d. 83   e. 45   f. 72
    g. 17   h. 84   i. 69   j. 28   k. 96   l. 49

4. Count in 5s as far as 100 (5, 10, 15, 20,... 100)
    Count in 6s as far as 100 (6, 12, 18, 24,... 96)

5. Emma has bought seven 88-page copies.
    How many pages has she altogether?

6. Tony has 3 photo albums. There are 56 photos
    in each album. How many photos does Tony have?

7. **Find half of each of these numbers:**
    a. 12   b. 16   c. 20   d. 22   e. 24   f. 30
    g. 42   h. 46   i. 66   j. 84   k. 90   l. 52

8. a. 2 x 7 = ☐   b. 2 x 3 = ☐   c. 6 x 8 = ☐
    d. 3 x 9 = ☐   e. 3 x 8 = ☐   f. 5 x 9 = ☐

9. a. 6 x 6 = ☐   b. 11 x 5 = ☐   c. 6 x 4 = ☐
    d. 8 x 2 = ☐   e. 8 x 6 = ☐   f. 7 x 3 = ☐

10. a. 8 x 4 = ☐   b. 9 x 1 = ☐   c. 8 x 8 = ☐
    d. 6 x 7 = ☐   e. 4 x 9 = ☐   f. 9 x 7 = ☐

11. a. 8 x 5 = ☐   b. 11 x 1 = ☐   c. 10 x 6 = ☐
    d. 7 x 9 = ☐   e. 12 x 7 = ☐   f. 12 x 5 = ☐

1. a. $63 \div 3 = \boxed{}$ b. $84 \div 4 = \boxed{}$ c. $75 \div 5 = \boxed{}$ d. $78 \div 6 = \boxed{}$

   e. $68 \div 4 = \boxed{}$ f. $95 \div 5 = \boxed{}$ g. $91 \div 7 = \boxed{}$ h. $98 \div 7 = \boxed{}$

2. **Try these (you may find remainders).**

   a. $53 \div 5 = \boxed{}$ b. $83 \div 8 = \boxed{}$ c. $76 \div 7 = \boxed{}$ d. $49 \div 4 = \boxed{}$

   e. $70 \div 6 = \boxed{}$ f. $83 \div 9 = \boxed{}$ g. $95 \div 7 = \boxed{}$ h. $75 \div 4 = \boxed{}$

   i. $60 \div 7 = \boxed{}$ j. $81 \div 9 = \boxed{}$ k. $96 \div 6 = \boxed{}$ l. $85 \div 7 = \boxed{}$

3. A baker used 6 trays to bake 96 cakes.
   Each tray held the same number of cakes.
   How many cakes did each tray hold?

4.  Barry was playing cards with his friends. A pack of cards contains 52 cards. He dealt 5 hands of cards, giving each person the same number of cards. If he gave each person as many cards as possible, how many cards had he left over?

5. How many bags of apples weighing 5 kilogrammes can I fill from a barrel containing 62 kilogrammes? How many kilogrammes of apples will be left over?

6.	a.	$14 \div 7 =$		b.	$21 \div 3 =$	c.	$48 \div 8 =$
	d.	$18 \div 9 =$		e.	$32 \div 8 =$	f.	$81 \div 9 =$
7.	a.	$18 \div 6 =$		b.	$35 \div 5 =$	c.	$36 \div 4 =$
	d.	$12 \div 2 =$		e.	$36 \div 6 =$	f.	$36 \div 3 =$
8.	a.	$16 \div 4 =$		b.	$12 \div 1 =$	c.	$56 \div 8 =$
	d.	$21 \div 7 =$		e.	$9 \div 9 =$	f.	$63 \div 7 =$
9.	a.	$25 \div 5 =$		b.	$27 \div 9 =$	c.	$28 \div 4 =$
	d.	$54 \div 9 =$		e.	$45 \div 9 =$	f.	$49 \div 7 =$

1. **Round these numbers to the nearest 10.**
   Example: 42 is nearer to 40 than 50.

   a. 21   b. 32   c. 59   d. 48   e. 13   f. 78

2. **Round these numbers to the nearest 100.**
   Example: 340 is nearer to 300 than 400.

   a. 430   b. 780   c. 910   d. 730   e. 110   f. 190

3. **What digital time does each clock face show?**

   a.   b.   c.   d.

   ┌──────────┐ ┌──────────┐ ┌──────────┐ ┌──────────┐
   └──────────┘ └──────────┘ └──────────┘ └──────────┘

4. **Write these amounts of money in €. Example: 132c = €1·32.**

   a. 145c   b. 198c   c. 458c   d. 784c   e. 903c   f. 111c

5. **Which is greater?**

   a. $\frac{1}{2}$ or $\frac{1}{4}$ b. $\frac{7}{8}$ or $\frac{1}{8}$ c. $\frac{3}{10}$ or $\frac{5}{10}$ d. $\frac{1}{6}$ or $\frac{1}{8}$

6. **Which is greater?**

   a. 0·3 or 0·4   b. 0·9 or 0·5   c. 0·5 or 0·2   d. 0·7 or 0·4

7. **What coins (1c, 2c, 5c, 10c, 20c, 50c) would you use to make these amounts?**
   Use as few coins as possible.

   a. 68c   b. 54c   c. 72c   d. 95c   e. 87c

   f. 81c   g. 79c   h. 52c   i. 62c   j. 82c

8. **Put in the correct signs (+ − x ÷).**

   a.   (4 ☐ 5) ☐ 6 = 15   b.   (2 ☐ 3) ☐ 4 = 24

   c.   (20 ☐ 9) ☐ 8 = 3   d.   (24 ☐ 3) ☐ 4 = 32

   e.   (12 ☐ 6) ☐ 3 = 6   f.   (7 ☐ 7) ☐ 14 = 0

1. **What number is shown on each place-value board?**

a.

H	T	U
1	2	5

b.

H	T	U

c.

H	T	U

d.

H	T	U

ONE THOUSAND

> 10 units = 1 rod
> 100 units = 10 rods = 1 flat

2. How many units could you swap for 1 flat?

3. How many units could you swap for 10 flats?

We call this number **one thousand**.

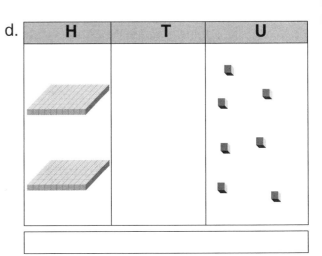

1	10	100	1,000
one	ten	hundred	thousand
unit	rod	flat	cube

We can put **10** hundreds (flats) together to make **1 cube**.

1. How many flats could you swap for **2 cubes**?

2. How many hundreds make up **2 thousand**?

3. How many flats could you swap for **3 cubes**?

4. How many hundreds make up **3 thousand**?

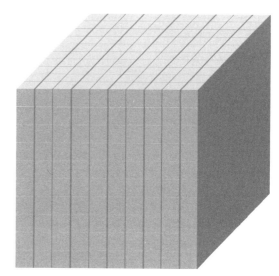

5. What number is shown on these place-value boards?

Thousands	H	T	U

Thousands	H	T	U

P 6. **Show these numbers on a place-value board using Base Ten blocks:**
   a. 1,234   b. 1,357   c. 1,450   d. 1,305   e. 1,087   f. 2,007

   g. 1,056   h. 1,310   i. 2,106   j. 1,005   k. 1,500   l. 2,400

Just for fun!
"If you had €3·56 in one pocket and €4·98 in the other pocket, what would you have?" the teacher asked Jimmy one day.
"Somebody else's trousers!" replied Jimmy.

Here is another way of showing thousands, hundreds, tens and units:

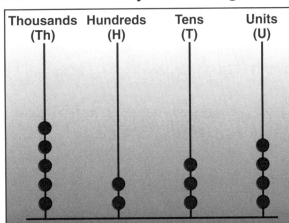

The number shown here is 5,234.

5,000 + 200 + 30 + 4

Five thousand, two hundred and thirty-four.

What number is shown by each of these pictures?

1. a.

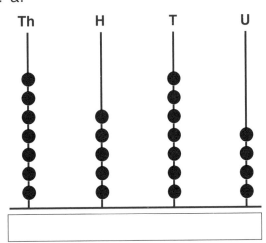

b.

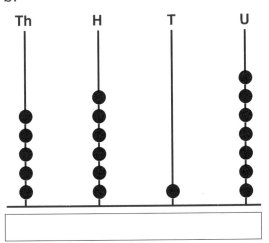

2. a.

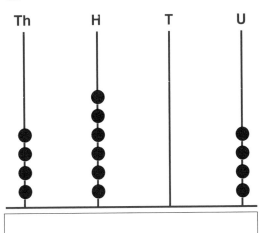

b.

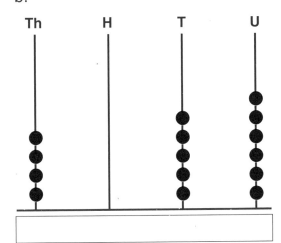

What number is shown by each of these pictures?

1. a. 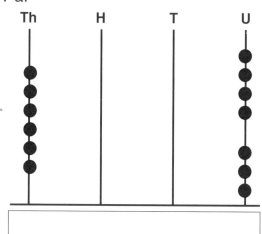   b.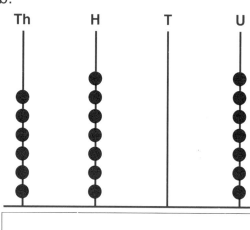

2. a. 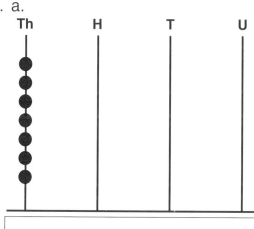   b.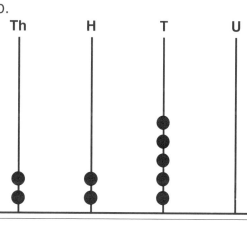

P 3. **Use your abacus sheet to show these numbers:**

a. 4,536   b. 5,671   c. 9,111   d. 2,335   e. 3,167   f. 4,336

g. 4,000   h. 6,045   i. 5,402   j. 1,001   k. 8,012   l. 3,305

4. **Write these numbers.**
   Example: Two thousand, one hundred and twenty-three = 2,123.
   a. Three thousand, eight hundred and ninety-seven.
   b. One thousand, seven hundred and fourteen.
   c. Five thousand, four hundred and thirty-two.
   d. Nine thousand, two hundred and four.
   e. Two thousand, six hundred and nine.
   f. Seven thousand and eighty-four.
   g. Four thousand and eleven.
   h. Eight thousand and three.

1. **Write each of these numbers in words.**
   Example: 1,013 = One thousand and thirteen.
   a. 2,114   b. 3,567   c. 9,058   d. 4,360   e. 4,003

2. **What number comes before each of these numbers?**
   a. 26   b. 100   c. 785   d. 1,440   e. 2,000   f. 3,010

3. **Write the number that comes after each of the following:**
   a. 76   b. 123   c. 269   d. 399   e. 809
   f. 1,000   g. 1,459   h. 2,099   i. 4,509   j. 9,309

4. **Which of these numbers is the greatest?**
   a. 2,345   3,567   or   4,573   b. 8,678   9,341   or   4,557
   c. 1,999   1,499   or   2,000   d. 3,001   2,998   or   1,990
   e. 8,103   8,013   or   8,310   f. 4,019   4,910   or   4,109

5. **Put each set of numbers in order starting with the smallest:**
   a. 6,000   4,000   2,000   b. 2,473   5,394   1,459
   c. 4,684   8,483   7,432   d. 3,333   3,033   3,330
   e. 6,158   6,851   6,581   f. 5,055   5,505   5,550

6. **What number comes next in each of these sequences?**
   a. 100   300   500   700   ____   b. 1,300   1,500   1,700   1,900   ____
   c. 2,310   2,330   2,350   2,370   ____   d. 6,244   6,248   6,252   6,256   ____
   e. 1,980   1,985   1,990   1,995   ____   f. 2,089   2,092   2,095   2,098   ____

THE FOX AND THE BEAR

When you're thinking about the **value** of a number, remember the story about the fox and the bear...

A fox and a bear planted a crop of corn. They agreed that when the corn grew the bear would take whatever was *below* the ground and the fox would take whatever was *above* the ground. Of course the bear ended up with something of **no value**. The next year, the bear said that he would take whatever was *above* the ground. However, the clever fox planted potatoes and, once again, the bear got something of **no value**.

DIGIT ORDER

1. **In which of these numbers has the digit 4 the greatest value?**

   a. 5,467 1,374 or 4,681   b. 5,114 6,425 or 7,145

   c. 1,243 304 or 5,432   d. 4,009 9,040 or 8,431

   e. 4,671 5,954 or 3,498   f. 456 4,079 or 3,034

2. **Write down all the numbers you can make from each set of digits.**

   a. 3, 4 and 9   b. 8, 3 and 5   c. 9, 8 and 7

   d. 1, 4 and 6   e. 2, 5 and 9   f. 1, 4 and 5

   g. 0, 6 and 7   h. 6, 6 and 5   i. 4, 4 and 8

   j. 3, 2, 7 and 8   k. 9, 6, 4 and 4   l. 6, 6, 7 and 7

3. **Make the greatest possible number from each set of digits.**
   Then make the smallest possible number.

   a. 3, 5, 6 and 2   b. 1, 1, 1 and 5   c. 6, 0, 0 and 8

   d. 4, 4, 7 and 7   e. 4, 5, 5 and 5   f. 3, 5, 9 and 9

   g. 3, 0, 9 and 4   h. 6, 4, 0 and 0   i. 4, 5, 0 and 4

4. **Ring the number that is nearer to 3,000.**

   a. 3,400 or 3,600   b. 3,900 or 3,750   c. 3,440 or 3,480

   d. 3,056 or 3,065   e. 3,010 or 3,001   f. 2,900 or 2,700

   g. 2,345 or 2,534   h. 2,690 or 2,790   i. 2,960 or 3,039

5. **Ring the number that is nearer to 5,000.**

   a. 4,600 or 4,660   b. 5,089 or 5,098   c. 4,996 or 4,969

   d. 5,001 or 5,010   e. 4,950 or 5,049   f. 5,113 or 4,890

ROUNDING

Round 3,200 to the nearest thousand.
Is it nearer to 3,000 or nearer to 4,000?
Numbers up to 3,499 are rounded to 3,000.
Numbers from 3,500 on are rounded to 4,000.

1. **Round each of these numbers to the nearest thousand:**
   a. 2,300   b. 3,900   c. 4,100   d. 9,200   e. 3,250   f. 4,750

   g. 7,999   h. 1,003   i. 2,463   j. 8,669   k.   779   l. 5,500

   m. 1,001   n. 1,999   o. 2,500   p.   900   q. 1,100   r. 4,440

COUNTING THE YEARS

2. What year is it now? How many digits does it have?

> There are 100 years in a century.
> There are 1,000 years in a millennium.

3. a. In what year were you born?
   b. Are there 4 digits in that year?

4. A year doesn't always have 4 digits.
   The Vikings landed on Lambay Island in the year AD 795.
   In what century was that?

5. A year might only have two digits. A volcano erupted in Italy in AD 79.
   In what century was that?

6. **A baby was born in 1999. How old will it be in each of these years?**
   a. 2012   b. 2015   c. 2019   d. 2032   e. 2049

7. **In what year will you celebrate your:**
   a. 12th birthday?   b. 21st birthday?

8. During a space movie the hero travels in time
   from the year AD 2540 to AD 2450. Did he
   travel forwards or backwards in time?

Unit 3 – Addition

1. a. $4 + 6 + 7 =$ ☐

   b. $3 + 5 + 9 =$ ☐

   c. $4 + 5 + 6 =$ ☐

   d. $9 + 8 + 4 =$ ☐

   e. $11 + 10 + 2 =$ ☐

   f. $12 + 12 + 6 =$ ☐

2. a. $4 + 9 + 3 =$ ☐

   b. $8 + 8 + 8 =$ ☐

   c. $9 + 7 + 5 =$ ☐

   d. $4 + 5 + 6 + 7 =$ ☐

   e. $3 + 5 + 7 + 9 =$ ☐

   f. $9 + 8 + 7 + 6 =$ ☐

3. a. $20 + 14 + 2 =$ ☐

   b. $30 + 12 + 5 =$ ☐

   c. $25 + 25 =$ ☐

   d. $41 + 53 =$ ☐

   e. $32 + 48 =$ ☐

   f. $26 + 35 =$ ☐

4. How much will I pay for 3 lollipops costing 12c, 14c and 20c?

5. How much will I pay for 2 pencils costing 21c each and a pen costing 22c?

6. If I read 13 pages on Monday, 14 pages on Tuesday and 17 pages on Wednesday, how many pages will I read altogether?

7. I have collected 240 cards. My friend gives me another 59. How many have I now?

8. There are 365 days in a year. How many days are there in a year and 2 weeks?

9. Barney eats 2 nuts on Sunday, 3 nuts on Monday, 4 nuts on Tuesday and so on. How many nuts will he eat in a week?

10.
a.	b.	c.	d.	e.	f.
23	34	45	73	621	253
+ 45	+ 46	+ 74	+ 84	+ 145	+ 382

11.
a.	b.	c.	d.	e.	f.
45	64	73	99	116	662
762	234	742	118	223	9
+ 111	+ 256	+ 118	+ 732	+ 364	+ 87

12. a. $23 + 45 + 56 =$ ☐   b. $45 + 64 + 42 =$ ☐

    c. $12 + 99 + 234 =$ ☐   d. $234 + 443 + 245 =$ ☐

    e. $246 + 551 + 119 =$ ☐   f. $331 + 332 + 333 =$ ☐

    g. $346 + 441 + 76 =$ ☐   h. $556 + 313 + 119 =$ ☐

    i. $447 + 228 + 5 =$ ☐   j. $112 + 249 + 390 =$ ☐

	Th	H	T	U
Thousands		4	7	5
		7	1	3
Sometimes when we add numbers, our answer is so big that it takes us into **thousands**.	+	8 $_1$	1 $_1$	8
	2,	0	0	6

1. a.
```
  465
+ 887
```
b.
```
  754
+ 526
```
c.
```
  823
+ 203
```
d.
```
  643
+ 357
```
e.
```
  743
+ 464
```
f.
```
  909
+  99
```

2. a.
```
  664
  118
+ 228
```
b.
```
  332
  229
+ 229
```
c.
```
   67
  202
+ 885
```
d.
```
  861
  330
+  69
```
e.
```
  336
  400
+ 373
```
f.
```
  716
   45
+ 831
```

3. a. 234 + 234 + 637 = ☐   b. 446 + 442 + 372 = ☐

   c. 40 + 345 + 792 = ☐   d. 754 + 382 + 80 = ☐

   e. 472 + 2 + 871 = ☐   f. 340 + 223 + 577 = ☐

   g. 999 + 999 + 999 = ☐   h. 560 + 660 + 760 = ☐

   i. 321 + 421 + 521 = ☐   j. 252 + 3 + 975 = ☐

	Th	H	T	U
Adding thousands				
Keep the units under the units.	4,	1	5	6
Keep the tens under the tens.	+ 3,	7	3 $_1$	8
Keep the hundreds under the hundreds.				
Keep the thousands under the thousands.	7,	8	9	4

4. a.
```
  2,423
+ 3,463
```
b.
```
  3,463
+ 4,372
```
c.
```
  2,371
+ 1,119
```
d.
```
  1,709
+ 3,229
```
e.
```
  2,352
+   334
```
f.
```
  5,372
+ 4,442
```

5. a.
```
  3,271
+ 3,445
```
b.
```
  2,330
+ 3,228
```
c.
```
    330
+ 3,227
```
d.
```
     45
+ 1,110
```
e.
```
  3,447
+     7
```
f.
```
  4,323
+ 3,226
```

1. a. 2,346   b. 2,667   c. 2,789   d. 1,332   e. 7,441   f. 2,222
       2,347   5,112   1,009   2,347   23   3,333
     + 2,348   +   456   + 3,552   + 3,224   + 1,334   + 4,444

2. a. 3,441   b. 2,445   c.   23   d. 5,433   e. 6,551   f. 2,114
       2,441   1,332   1,345   7   34   1,000
     + 2,441   + 3,667   + 5,441   + 2,441   +   345   +   78

3. A baker baked 313 buns on Monday, 440 buns on Tuesday and 398 buns on Wednesday. How many buns did he bake altogether?

4.  A car travelled 1,229 kilometres in July, 2,334 kilometres in August and 2,226 kilometres in September. How many kilometres did it travel altogether?

5. a. 2,364 + 4,211 + 1,551 = ☐   b. 2,334 + 3,002 + 2,667 = ☐

   c. 3,334 + 3 + 2,335 = ☐   d. 3,664 + 34 + 3,119 = ☐

   e. 56 + 5,993 + 678 = ☐   f. 9 + 8,881 + 456 = ☐

6. A factory sold 1,556 litres of red paint, 1,882 litres of blue paint and 1,931 litres of yellow paint to a shop last year. How many litres of paint did it sell altogether?

7. A library has 7,113 books in English, 1,442 books in Irish, 554 books in French and 57 books in German. It has no books in any other language. How many books are in the library?

PUZZLE POWER

A farmer was on his way home from the market one day. He had with him a fox, a goose and a bag of corn. He reached a river that he had to cross. Unfortunately, there was only one small boat and he could only carry across his belongings one by one. The trouble was that if he left the goose alone with the corn, the goose would eat the corn, and if he left the fox alone with the goose, the fox would eat the goose. Can you help to solve his problem?

19

Make a **wild guess**:
How many stars are in the box? ☐

Now **estimate**:
How many stars are in the box? ☐

Now **count**:
How many stars are in the box? ☐

Were your two answers the same or almost the same? Is it better to make an **estimate** or a **wild guess**?

Answer the following:

Remember!
An estimate is a **sensible guess!**

1. Mum bought a skirt for her sister's birthday. She couldn't remember her sister's exact size but she knew she was a bit smaller than herself. Mum bought a size smaller than she would buy for herself. Was this a wild guess or an estimate?

2. Jack was the first to buy a ticket in the raffle. He could choose any ticket from the book. He chose number 792. Was this a wild guess or an estimate?

3. Dad bakes bread every Saturday. Last Saturday he dropped the kitchen scales on the floor and they broke. He needed to use 200 grammes of flour. He poured what he thought was 200 grammes into a bowl. Was this a wild guess or an estimate?

4. Jim always leaves for school when he hears the news at half past eight on the radio. Yesterday he forgot his watch and on the way to school his friend asked him the time. Jim thought for a moment and said, "I'm not exactly sure but it's about a quarter to nine." Was this a wild guess or an estimate?

5. Write two examples of guessing.

6. Write two examples of estimating.

7. **A museum held an Aztec exhibition. It was open every day except Monday.**
   a. On Tuesday it had 76 visitors, on Wednesday it had 88 visitors and on Thursday it had 79 visitors. How many people would you expect to visit the exhibition on Friday: 8, 18, 80 or 800?
   b. On Saturday it had 673 visitors. Why do you think so many visited on Saturday?
   c. How many visitors might you expect on Sunday: 8, 18, 80 or 800?

Rounding helps us to estimate answers, especially when the numbers are big.
- ■ If the numbers are **less than 100**, round them to the **nearest 10**.
- ■ If the numbers are **between 100 and 1,000**, round them to the **nearest 100**.
- ■ If the numbers are **greater than 1,000**, round them to the **nearest 1,000**.

Do **not** work out the **exact** answers on this page.

1. Estimate the answers to these sums by rounding the numbers to the **nearest 10** and adding.
   Example: 23 + 32 + 46
   20 + 30 + 50 = **100**

   a. 22 + 27 =

   b. 38 + 68 =

   c. 74 + 88 =

   d. 41 + 52 + 59 =

   e. 58 + 34 + 27 =

   f. 48 + 86 + 52 =

2. Estimate the answers to these sums by rounding the numbers to the **nearest 100** and adding.
   Example: 123 + 432 + 846
   100 + 400 + 800 = **1,300**

   a. 174 + 242 =

   b. 303 + 588 =

   c. 258 + 412 =

   d. 111 + 661 =

   e. 148 + 458 =

   f. 237 + 261 =

   g. 256 + 911 + 1 =

   h. 9 + 619 + 139 =

   i. 482 + 311 + 986 =

   j. 537 + 249 + 812 =

   k. 625 + 205 + 382 =

   l. 419 + 396 + 710 =

3.  Dave went shopping last Tuesday and into his basket he put four items which cost €1·91, €2·34, €4·67 and €1·63. In his pocket he had a €10 note. Do you think he had enough money with him to pay for his shopping?

1. Estimate the answers to these sums by rounding to the **nearest 1,000** and adding.

   Example: 2,331 + 3,724
                 2,000 + 4,000 = **6,000**

   a. 2,222 + 2,222 = ☐   b. 2,433 + 6,813 = ☐

   c. 3,710 + 3,220 = ☐   d. 3,873 + 4,667 = ☐

   e. 2,883 + 3,391 = ☐   f. 5,771 + 1,999 = ☐

   g. 2,364 + 3,573 + 1,071 = ☐   h. 4,991 + 1,113 + 2,669 = ☐

2. Linda went to the library on Monday and while she was there she heard the librarian saying that there were:

   2,460 books in the children's section,
   4,678 books in the adult section and
   1,778 books in the reference section.

   Estimate how many books were in the three sections altogether.
   Now work out the exact answer and see how close your estimate was.

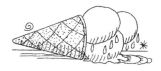

3. Here are the attendance figures at some football matches:

   a. 1,222   b. 1,441   c. 997   d. 5,889

   Estimate how many people altogether attended the four matches.
   Now work out the exact answer.
   Why do you think so many people went to match **d**?

4. The population of Oldtown is 3,225. The population of Newtown is 1,886 more than that of Oldtown. Estimate the total population of the two towns and then work out the exact answer.

5. 3,117 people went to a semi-final. There were 1,225 more than that at the final. Estimate how many people altogether attended the matches and then work out the exact answer.

6. Mr Snowman sold 1,334 ice creams during the summer.
   Mr Frosty sold 776 more ice creams than Mr Snowman.
   Estimate and then work out how many ice creams they sold between them.

PUZZLE POWER

In this sum the letters X, Y and Z stand for three different digits.   X X
Can you figure out what each letter stands for?   + Y Y
            Z Y Z

■ You may use your calculator whenever you see this symbol. A calculator is very useful for adding large numbers. It works out the answer very quickly and is never wrong. Of course you have to press the right buttons in the first place! Remember that your brain is far better than any machine or computer.

■ We call the buttons on the calculator, **keys**.

■ If you see a number or a symbol in a box like this you press that key on your calculator.

■ Turn your calculator on by pressing:

■ Practise pressing the keys. Key in the number of your house.

■ To clear this away press:

■ Key in your telephone number or any other numbers that come to mind.

PUZZLE POWER

Press 5 3 0 4 5   You'll find something you wear on your feet.

Press 5 3 7 0 4   You might have these in your pockets.

Of course you have to turn the calculator upside down to see the answers! See if you can form any other words.

1. Let's use the calculator to find the answers to easy sums.

Press   When you press the 'equals' symbol your answer appears.

Press **C** to clear your screen. Try lots of these.

2. Now let's try a much harder one: 4,557 + 3,091.

Press

You should find the answer 7,648 appearing instantly on your screen.

PUZZLE POWER

There was a young man from Bengal,
Who was asked to a fancy dress ball,
He murmured, "I'll risk it,
I'll go as a biscuit,"

— — — — — — — — — — !

Decode the last line of the limerick by working out the answer to each question.
Wherever you see your answer in the code-grid, put in whichever letter
is beside the question. Answers might appear more than once.
The first one is done for you:

U 4,557 + 3,091 = 7,648   T 5,588 + 3,266 =   I 2,500 + 4,886 =
N 3,175 + 1,366 =   G 1,599 + 4,747 =   B 3,939 + 2,828 =
A 7,993 + 1,884 =   O 338 + 2,489   =   E 3,158 + 6,339 =
L 3,558 + 2,545 =   M 7,763 + 2,145 =   H 1,456 + 3,545 =
P 2,584 + 4,771 =   D 3,377 + 4,789 =

	U								
6,767	7,648	8,854		9,877			8,166	2,827	6,346

								U	
9,877	8,854	9,497		5,001	7,386	9,908		7,648	7,355

7,386	4,541		8,854	5,001	9,497		5,001	9,877	6,103	6,103

1.
a. 9 − 7 = ☐
b. 10 − 3 = ☐
c. 9 − 2 = ☐
d. 8 − 8 = ☐
e. 6 − 0 = ☐
f. 13 − 4 = ☐
g. 15 − 3 = ☐
h. 20 − 11 = ☐
i. 22 − 9 = ☐
j. 17 − 2 = ☐

2.
a. 12 − ☐ = 5
b. 14 − ☐ = 2
c. 20 − ☐ = 5
d. 17 − ☐ = 8
e. 23 − ☐ = 19
f. 25 − ☐ = 25
g. 30 − ☐ = 0
h. 27 − ☐ = 24
i. 32 − ☐ = 18
j. 44 − ☐ = 26

3.
a. ☐ − 9 = 3
b. ☐ − 7 = 2
c. ☐ − 5 = 6
d. ☐ − 6 = 0
e. ☐ − 12 = 12
f. ☐ − 14 = 14
g. ☐ − 23 = 20
h. ☐ − 17 = 13
i. ☐ − 25 = 50
j. ☐ − 37 = 32

Example:

```
            H  T  U
  9 6 7     9 ⁵6̸ ¹7
− 2 2 8    − 2  2  8
            7  3  9
```

4.
a. 48 − 25
b. 67 − 42
c. 99 − 37
d. 86 − 38
e. 45 − 29
f. 82 − 17

5.
a. 259 − 127
b. 283 − 167
c. 192 − 88
d. 557 − 183
e. 482 − 291
f. 813 − 341

6.
a. 742 − 155
b. 851 − 277
c. 741 − 288
d. 551 − 389
e. 950 − 204
f. 831 − 266

7. A newsagent had 613 newspapers. He sold 597 of them. How many had he left?

8. A soccer team scored 126 goals last year. They scored 28 goals less this year. How many goals did they score this year?

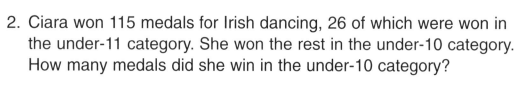

1. Uncle Ned is saving petrol tokens. He needs 360 tokens to get a CD player. He has collected 276 tokens. How many more does he need?

2. Ciara won 115 medals for Irish dancing, 26 of which were won in the under-11 category. She won the rest in the under-10 category. How many medals did she win in the under-10 category?

3. Colm's book should have 340 pages but the last two chapters are missing. The second last chapter had 18 pages and the last one had 24 pages. How many pages are actually in Colm's book?

4. a. 348 – 129 = ☐   b. 628 – 597 = ☐   c. 655 – 249 = ☐

    d. 748 – 129 = ☐   e. 846 – 648 = ☐   f. 422 – 391 = ☐

5. a. 345 – 119 = ☐   b. 446 – 229 = ☐   c. 751 – 159 = ☐

    d. 447 – 338 = ☐   e. 318 – 189 = ☐   f. 711 – 665 = ☐

Another example:

$$
\begin{array}{r}
\text{H T U} \\
{}^{2}3\ {}^{9}0\ {}^{1}7 \\
-\ 1\ 3\ 9 \\
\hline
1\ 6\ 8 \\
\end{array}
$$

6. a. 804   b. 703   c. 707   d. 601   e. 500   f. 901
    – 236   – 128   – 559   – 153   – 244   – 736

7. a. 701   b. 908   c. 300   d. 507   e. 601   f. 901
    – 546   – 619   – 155   – 148   – 348   – 736

8. A school was open for 108 days between January and June. If it rained on 36 of those days, on how many school days did it not rain?

9. A shop had 205 customers one day. 92 of these were men, 86 were women and the rest were children. How many children visited the shop that day?

Example:

	Th	H	T	U			Th	H	T	U
	9,	8	5	4			9,	⁷8	¹5	4
−	6,	3	7	2		−	6,	3	7	2
							3,	4	8	2

1.
  a. 9,753
     − 1,235

  b. 8,553
     − 2,337

  c. 7,552
     − 4,261

  d. 7,358
     − 2,519

  e. 8,457
     − 2,681

  f. 7,551
     − 3,891

2.
  a. 8,631
     − 2,799

  b. 7,401
     − 2,559

  c. 8,033
     − 3,247

  d. 9,012
     − 2,101

  e. 6,803
     − 3,517

  f. 5,101
     − 1,353

3. a. 3,208 − 1,445 = ☐   b. 5,028 − 2,339 = ☐   c. 8,307 − 2,338 = ☐

4. a. 8,059 − 1,588 = ☐   b. 5,078 − 3,228 = ☐   c. 7,029 − 5,555 = ☐

5. A warehouse holds 2,309 chairs. If 679 of them are taken out, how many are left?

6. A gallery had 1,056 paintings. Of these paintings, 312 were sold. A further 444 were bought. How many paintings has the gallery now?

Example:

	Th	H	T	U			Th	H	T	U
	4,	0	0	5			³4,	⁹0	⁹0	¹5
−	1,	2	3	9		−	1,	2	3	9
							2,	7	6	6

7.
  a. 6,004
     − 4,226

  b. 6,005
     − 3,448

  c. 9,003
     − 2,733

  d. 8,001
     − 7,552

  e. 3,006
     − 1,445

  f. 7,002
     − 6,226

8.
  a. 8,005
     − 3,555

  b 7,004
     − 5,447

  c. 5,005
     − 3,662

  d. 2,000
     − 557

  e. 8,000
     − 2,333

  f. 6,000
     − 4,662

1. There were 1,446 cars in a car park one morning.
During the lunch hour 569 of them left.
How many remained?

2.  A dealer bought 842 boxes of fruit. She sold 793 of them. How many had she left?

3. Emily won €2,468. She gave €1,469 of it away.
How much had she left?

4. How many years are there between 1492 and 1776?

5. A woman was born in 1972. How old is she now?

6. Alan has a collection of 1,244 stamps. How many
more stamps does he need to reach 2,000?

7. Mr Fox has €2,004 in the bank. Mr Murphy has €1,668 in the post office.
How much more money has Mr Fox than Mr Murphy?

8. A library holds 9,807 books. Of these, 2,559 are out on loan.
How many books are still in the library?

9. An archer needs to score 1,231 points or higher to
win a competition. He is only allowed to shoot three
more arrows. The most he can score with one arrow
is 10 points. Can he win the competition if his score
at the moment is 1,199?

BRACKETS

First work out the answer to the question **inside** the brackets.	$52 - (8 + 24)$ $52 - \quad 32 \quad = 20$

10.

a. $20 - (5 + 4) =$ ☐
b. $30 - (7 + 8) =$ ☐
c. $40 - (9 + 6) =$ ☐
d. $50 - (8 + 7) =$ ☐
e. $21 - (9 + 8) =$ ☐
f. $29 - (11 + 11) =$ ☐
g. $35 - (23 + 12) =$ ☐

11.

a. $160 - (23 + 55) =$ ☐
b. $142 - (16 + 62) =$ ☐
c. $347 - (82 + 29) =$ ☐
d. $434 - (210 + 144) =$ ☐
e. $371 + (159 - 60) =$ ☐
f. $200 + (143 - 25) =$ ☐
g. $135 + (400 - 148) =$ ☐

1. A jam factory ordered 4,226 kilogrammes of sugar. A lorry brought 1,005 kilogrammes on Monday and 998 kilogrammes on Tuesday. How much more sugar does the lorry need to bring?

2.  An ice cream factory needed 9,846 litres of cream. Butler's creamery supplied 3,447 litres and Whelan's creamery supplied 3,435 litres. How many more litres did the factory need?

3. A woman earned €1,142 in June and €1,168 in July. She spent €1,984. How much had she left?

4.  A forest had 8,196 Christmas trees. The owner cut down 2,115 trees and he planted 1,998 trees. How many trees are there in the forest now?

5. There were 2,164 visitors to a castle in spring, 3,223 visitors in summer and 1,860 visitors in autumn. Each visitor was charged €1. A new roof for the castle would cost €8,000. Was enough money collected to pay for a new roof? If not, how much more was needed?

6. A car needs to be checked every time it travels 9,000 kilometres. If a sales representative travelled 3,554 kilometres in March and 4,117 kilometres in April, how many more kilometres can the car travel before it needs to be checked?

7. In a park there were 2,169 trees. During a storm 283 of these were blown down. The owner later planted 312 new trees. How many trees are now in the park?

8. A newsagent needs to sell 6,000 newspapers a week. Last week he sold 951 on Monday, 874 on Tuesday, 880 on Wednesday and 1,003 on Thursday. How many does he need to sell on Friday, Saturday and Sunday?

9. On St Patrick's Day there were 4,008 people at a parade. Of these, 1,220 were men, 1,013 were women and the rest were children. How many were children?

10. A woman won €1,000. She spent €234 in May and she spent €46 more than that in June. How much has she left?

Do **not** work out the exact answers!

1. **Estimate the answers. Round to the nearest 100 and subtract.**
   Example: 872 – 523
   900 – 500 = 400

   a. 679 – 311 = ☐   b. 489 – 111 = ☐   c. 524 – 222 = ☐

   d. 778 – 399 = ☐   e. 929 – 101 = ☐   f. 444 – 289 = ☐

   g. 730 – 511 = ☐   h. 304 – 198 = ☐   i. 605 – 270 = ☐

2. **Estimate the answers. Round to the nearest 1,000 and subtract.**
   Example: 7,664 – 3333
   8,000 – 3,000 = 5,000

   a. 6,112 – 3,131 = ☐   b. 8,779 – 2,001 = ☐

   c. 9,003 – 1,345 = ☐   d. 9,335 – 6,778 = ☐

   e. 6,710 – 5,889 = ☐   f. 3,445 – 2,998 = ☐

   g. 3,005 – 1,111 = ☐   h. 6,998 – 4,010 = ☐

PUZZLE POWER

A man had 7 silver rings that were linked together like this.
His landlady came to him one day and asked for
his rent. Alas, the man had no money but he offered to
give her a silver ring every month he stayed.
The landlady agreed. However, she made one
strange request. "You may only break one of
the rings," she said, "and you must stay here for
7 months." Which ring did he break so that the landlady had 1 ring after
1 month, 2 rings after 2 months, 3 rings after 3 months, and so on?

6,109 – 3,482

Press

You should find the answer 2,627 appearing on your screen.

1. a. 456 – 234 = ☐   b. 786 – 245 = ☐

   c. 556 – 130 = ☐   d. 980 – 235 = ☐

   e. 876 – 664 = ☐   f. 347 – 234 = ☐

   g. 4,567 – 1,246 = ☐   h. 6,772 – 2,558 = ☐

   i. 9,556 – 1,255 = ☐   j. 8,002 – 1,445 = ☐

   k. 7,584 – 234 = ☐   l. 5,667 – 1,445 = ☐

PUZZLE POWER

**What did the doctor say when her patient said,
"Doctor, I feel like a spoon"?**

Decode the doctor's reply by answering each question.
You may use a calculator. Wherever you see your answer in the
code-grid, put in whichever letter is beside the question.
Answers might appear more than once. The first one is done
for you.

A   8,742 – 3,466 = 5,276   W   8,550 – 7,999 =
R   7,129 – 4,528 =   I   7,000 – 5,662 =
D   6,583 – 3,462 =   N   5,004 – 3,229 =
H   8,110 – 4,567 =   O   6,109 – 3,677 =
E   7,668 – 4,060 =   S   8,100 – 4,379 =
T   9,005 – 5,773 =

3,721	1,338	3,232		3,121	2,432	551	1,775

						A		
3,232	3,543	3,608	2,601	3,608		5,276	1,775	3,121

3,121	2,432	1,775	3,232		3,721	3,232	1,338	2,601

Make up your own sum code.
Think of a joke and see if a partner can decode the answer.

Unit 5 – Lines and Angles

Parallel lines are lines that never meet.
They are always the same distance apart.

1. **Look at these lines. Tick the parallel sets of lines.**

a.

b.

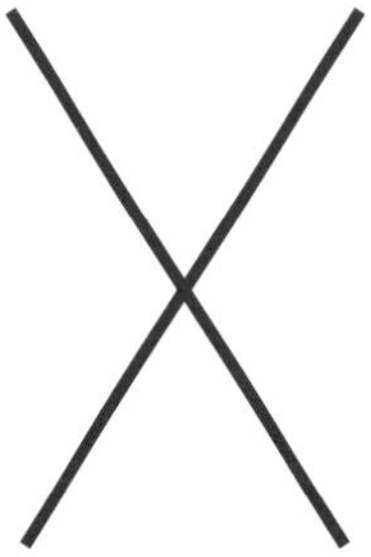

c.

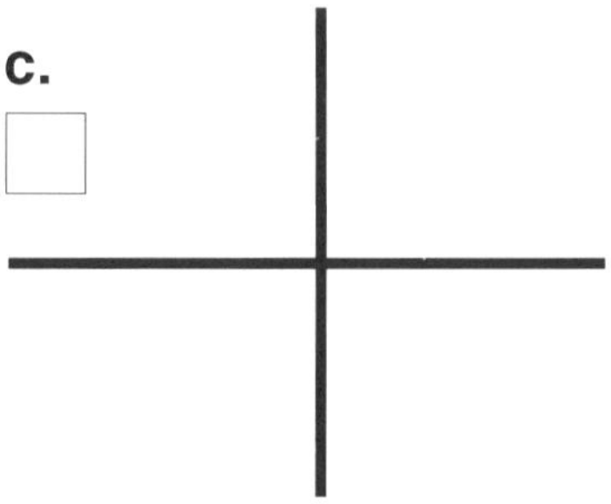

d.

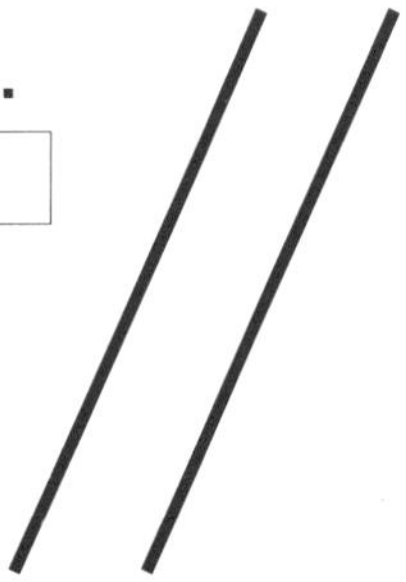

e.

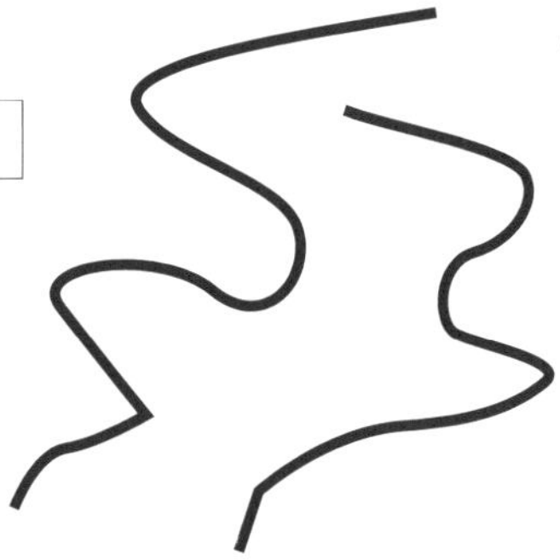

f.

g.

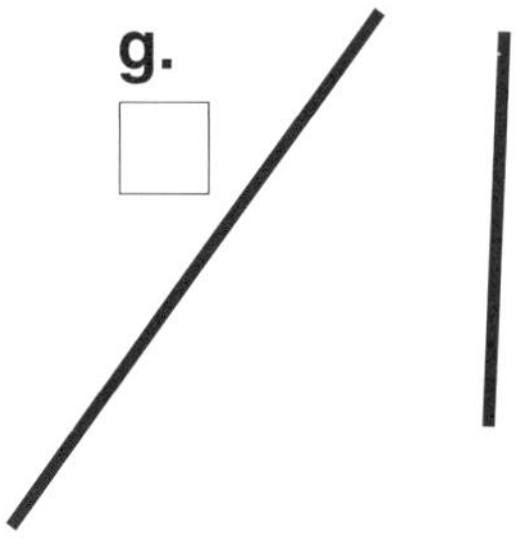

2. Write down 5 examples of where you might see parallel lines in the world around you.

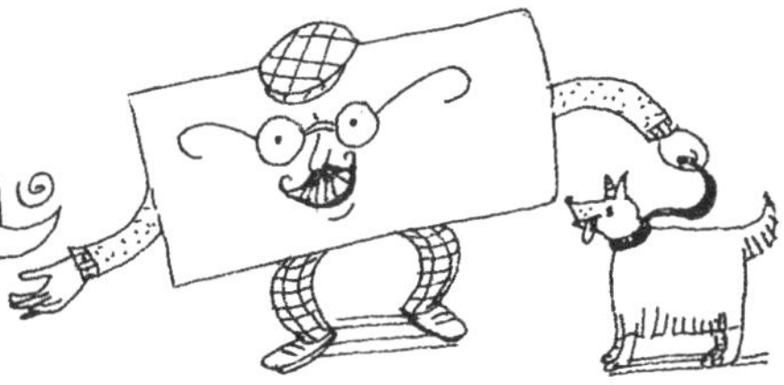

RIGHT ANGLES

3. **How many right angles can you see in each of these drawings?**

a.

b.

c.

d.

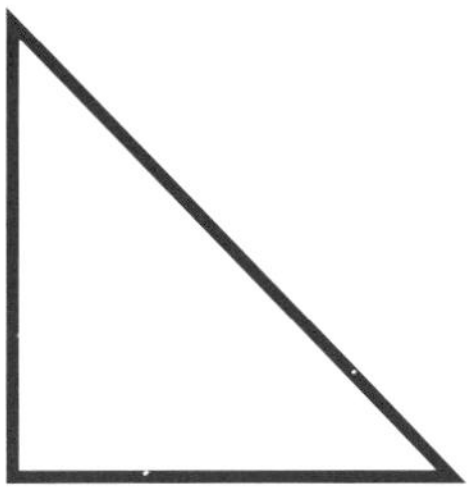

e.

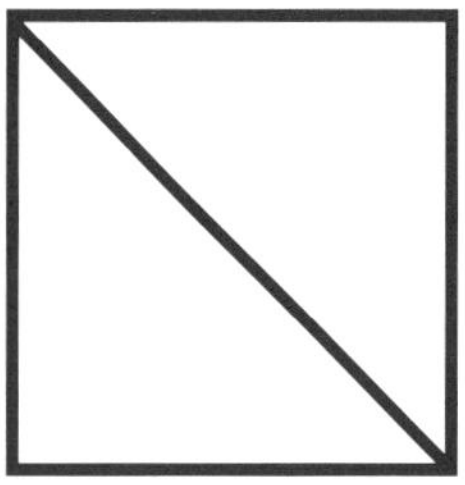

f.

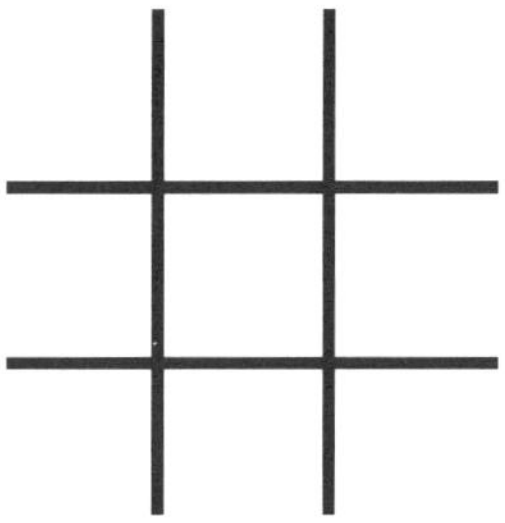

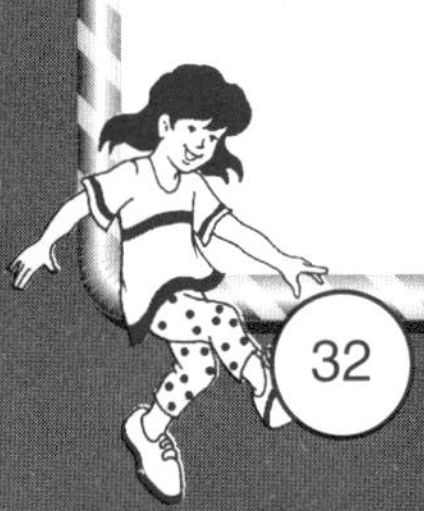

When two lines meet and form a right angle they are said to be **perpendicular** to each other.

1. **Look at these pairs of lines. Tick the ones that are perpendicular.**

   a. ☐   b. ☐   c. ☐   d. ☐   e.

2. **Tick the lines that are perpendicular to Line M.**

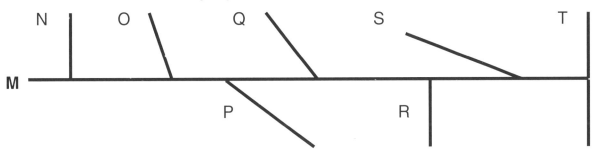

3. Name 4 places in the world around you where you can see perpendicular lines. Example: The wall of the classroom is perpendicular to the floor.

4. **Colour in the shapes that have perpendicular lines.**

   a.   b.   c.   d.   e.   f.

5. Could two parallel lines ever be perpendicular to each other?

6. Draw a line and call it Line A. Draw a line perpendicular to Line A and call it Line B. Now draw a third line perpendicular to Line B and call it Line C. Are Line A and Line C parallel or perpendicular?

7. Which of these symbols have perpendicular lines?

Y + K M A E L # < =

Imagine that you're on a beach looking out to sea. Far in the distance it *seems* that the sea and the sky meet. That line where they seem to meet is called the **horizon**.

So a **horizontal** line lies flat like this: ————

A **vertical** line stands up straight like this: |

1. Are you horizontal or vertical when you're in bed?

2. Is a soldier on duty horizontal or vertical?

3. **Look at this picture of a door and answer these questions:**

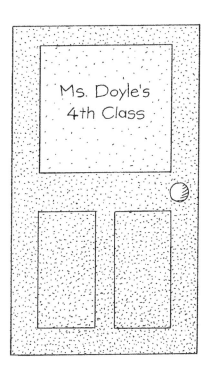

Ms. Doyle's 4th Class

   a. How many vertical lines can you see?
   b. How many horizontal lines can you see?
   c. Are all the vertical lines parallel?
   d. Are all the horizontal lines parallel?
   e. Are the vertical lines parallel to the horizontal lines?
   f. Is the door to your classroom vertical or horizontal?
   g. What kind of door might be placed in a horizontal position?

4. **Write down three other examples of:**
   a. vertical lines in the world around you.
   b. horizontal lines in the world around you.

5. What instrument does a builder use to make sure the blocks are horizontal?

6. **Make a plumb line.**
   Tie a weight to a piece of string and let it dangle. When it settles the string is vertical. Use it to check that things such as pictures on the wall are vertical.
   Think of a few other uses for a plumb line.

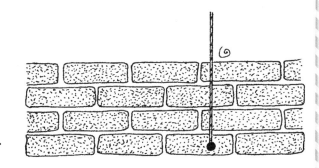

A set square is a triangular instrument shaped like this→ or this→

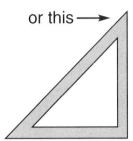

We can use a set square to draw **perpendicular** lines and **parallel** lines.

1. Draw a straight line with your ruler. It doesn't matter how long it is but about 10cm will be fine. Use a pencil.

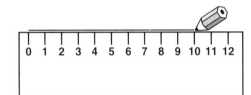

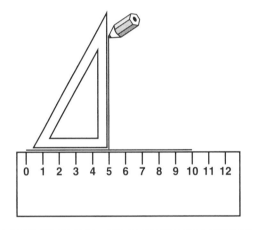

2. Put your set square alongside your ruler as you see in the picture. Draw a straight line. Your two lines are **perpendicular**.

4. Slide the set square along the ruler. (Be careful not to let your ruler move.) Draw another line. Always use a pencil.

3. Draw a line here.

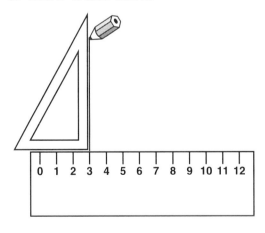

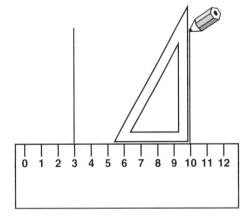

The further you drag your set square along the ruler, the further apart your **parallel** lines will be. You can draw as many parallel lines in this way as you want. Experiment!

Lines that cross are said to **intersect**. In America a crossroads is called an **intersection**.
When lines intersect they form angles.

An angle that is **less than** a right angle is said to be **acute** (sharp).
An angle that is **greater than** a right angle is said to be **obtuse**.

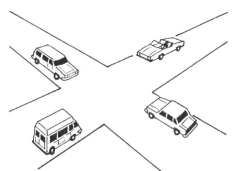

Acute   **Obtuse**

1. **Say whether each of these angles is a right angle, an acute angle, or an obtuse angle.**

a.

b.

c.

d.

e.

f.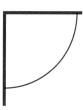

g.

h.

i.

j.

k.

l.

1. Draw 4 acute angles and 4 obtuse angles.

2. Use your ruler and set square to draw 4 right angles.

Put each of these sets of 4 angles in order. Start with the smallest.

3. **a.**  **b.**  **c.**  **d.**

4. **a.**  **b.**  **c.** **d.**

5. **a.**  **b.** **c.**  **d.**

6. **a.**  **b.**  **c.** 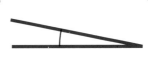 **d.**

How many **right angles** can you see in this drawing?

How many **squares** can you see in this drawing?

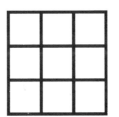

1. **What type of angle are the hands of each clock making?**

   a.
   b.
   c.
   d.

   e.
   f.
   g.
   h.

2. **Will the hands of each clock still make the same type of angle 10 minutes later?**

3. **Use the diagram to answer the questions.**

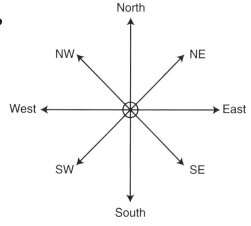

a.  Emma was facing north. She turned through one right angle in a clockwise direction. In what direction does she now face?

b. Trevor was facing south. He turned through 2 right angles in a clockwise direction. In what direction does he now face? If he had turned through 2 right angles in an anticlockwise direction where would he face?

c.  Rachel faced north-east. She turned in a clockwise direction and now faces south-east. Through how many right angles did she turn?

Let's Look Back (2)

1.
- a. 9 + 9 = ☐
- b. 8 + 13 = ☐
- c. 13 + 13 = ☐
- d. 15 + 15 = ☐
- e. 21 + 35 = ☐
- f. 26 + 36 = ☐

2.
- a. 13 − 7 = ☐
- b. 15 − 6 = ☐
- c. 22 − 13 = ☐
- d. 25 − 16 = ☐
- e. 40 − 18 = ☐
- f. 70 − 51 = ☐

3. Write this number in digits: Eight thousand and six.

4. What number comes next: 987, 991, 995, 999, _____?

5. Which is greatest: 5,100   5,099   5,002   or   5,089?

6. If there are 41 books on the bottom shelf, 37 books on the middle shelf and 21 books on the top shelf, how many books are there altogether?

7. What type of angle is this?

8. **True or false?**
   "Horizontal lines are always perpendicular to vertical lines."

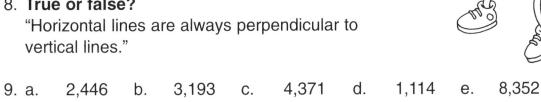

9. a.   2,446   b.   3,193   c.   4,371   d.   1,114   e.   8,352
      + 3,563   + 4,882   + 1,447   + 385   +   33

10. a.   8,557   b.   7,664   c.   5,205   d.   2,023   e.   8,004
       − 3,575   − 5,417   − 3,627   − 1,557   − 2,118

11. A shop had 1,334 customers on Monday, 1,440 on Tuesday, 998 on Wednesday, 1,007 on Thursday and 1,559 on Friday. How many customers went to the shop altogether that week?

12. How much does a woman need to borrow for a car that costs €9,000 if she has saved €2,500 and her present car is worth €3,600?

1. Make the **greatest** number you can using the digits 3, 8, 9 and 1.

2. Make the **smallest** number you can using the digits 3, 8, 9 and 1.

3. Which of these numbers is nearest to 7,000: 6,880 or 7,121 or 7,335?

4. Which of these letters have **both** perpendicular and parallel lines?

H K L M N T E V X F

5. What kind of angle do the hands of a clock form at exactly 9 o'clock?

6. **How much for:**
   a. A maths copy for 29c, a ruler for 15c and a pen for 21c?
   b. A bar for 35c, a drink for 45c and chewing gum for 15c?
   c. Six lollies at 5c each and a lucky bag for 19c?
   d. Seven 3c sweets and an ice cream for 38c?
   e. Half a dozen 4c cool pops and a single of chips for 75c?
   f. What change would I get from €1·00 in each of the above?

> **Remember!** Work out the sum **inside the brackets** first.

7. a. $(2{,}556 + 3{,}220) - 4{,}551 = \boxed{}$ b. $(7{,}555 - 2{,}119) + 1{,}229 = \boxed{}$

8. a. $(3{,}229 + 5{,}228) - 3{,}448 = \boxed{}$ b. $(9{,}555 - 2{,}338) + 668 = \boxed{}$

9. a. $(4{,}444 + 2{,}313) - 6{,}118 = \boxed{}$ b. $(7{,}023 - 6{,}119) + 2{,}338 = \boxed{}$

10. A dictionary had 8,446 pages and was so big it had to be divided into three separate books. Volume 1 had 2,776 pages and volume 2 had 2,886 pages. How many pages were in volume 3?

11. Take 2,335 from the sum of 1,385 and 6,119.

12. Add 1,665 to the difference between 6,509 and 5,998.

13. Take the difference between 2,335 and 3,664 from the sum of those two numbers.

PONTOON 100

This is an estimating game. Your task is to estimate whether the answer to each question is less than or more than 100. Round the numbers to the nearest ten.

Less than 100	More than 100
	89 + 56

89 + 56	77 + 50	13 + 61	61 + 51	78 + 14
42 + 53	66 + 43	58 + 27	35 + 69	22 + 87
123 − 11	156 − 88	168 − 42	199 − 67	177 − 51

When you have finished, check your estimates.

PUZZLE POWER

1. **Work out what the letters stand for in each of the following:**
   a. 52 W in a Y
   b. 4 S on a S
   c. 7 C in the R
   d. 32 C in I
   e. 24 H in a D
   f. 18 H on a G C
   g. 64 S on a C B
   h. 12 in a D
   i. S W and the 7 D
   j. 9 P in the S S

   Clue: 7 D in a W
   Answer: 7 Days in a Week

2. **What number am I?**
   a. I am an even number. I am less than 20 and greater than 14. If you divide me by 8 you will get a remainder.

   b. I am an odd number. I am between 20 and 30. When you are my age you will have a big party. Written backwards I am a dozen.

   c. I have three digits. You can write me backwards and I won't change. Some people say that my first two digits are an unlucky number.

   d. I have three digits. All my digits are the same. When you add my three digits together you get 12.

   e. I have 4 digits. Each of my first three digits is one greater than the digit to the right of it. My third digit is 5.

   Just for fun!
   Q. Why was 6 sad at dinner?
   A. Because 7 8 9!

1.
a. 4 x 5 =
b. 2 x 4 =
c. 3 x 5 =
d. 5 x 2 =
e. 9 x 3 =
f. 7 x 7 =
g. 8 x 4 =
h. 7 x 2 =
i. 5 x 6 =
j. 9 x 9 =

2.
a. 7 x 8 =
b. 6 x 6 =
c. 9 x 4 =
d. 8 x 6 =
e. 7 x 1 =
f. 9 x 7 =
g. 8 x 0 =
h. 5 x 5 =
i. 7 x 8 =
j. 4 x 11 =

3.
a. ☐ x 3 = 12
b. ☐ x 4 = 16
c. ☐ x 5 = 20
d. ☐ x 6 = 30
e. ☐ x 8 = 48
f. 7 x ☐ = 21
g. 5 x ☐ = 45
h. 9 x ☐ = 63
i. 8 x ☐ = 40
j. 6 x ☐ = 42

4. A car has 4 wheels and a spare wheel.
   How many wheels have 9 cars?

5.  A minibus has 10 seats. The driver uses one of these. How many passengers can the driver bring to school if he makes 4 trips?

6. A pen set has 3 blue pens, 3 black pens and 2 red pens.
   How many pens are there in 8 sets of pens?

7. The Queen of Howmanishus has 41 pairs of shoes.
   How many shoes has she?

8. How many in 3 dozen?

9. There are 100 years in a century.
   How many years are there in 3 centuries?

10. At Anna's birthday party there were 7 six-packs of lemonade. How many bottles of lemonade is this?

11.  It was the triplets' 11th birthday party. They had one cake between them. How many candles were on it if they each had a candle for every year of their lives?

1. a. 21   b. 31   c. 42   d. 33   e. 42   f. 50
        x 3   x 2   x 4   x 3   x 5   x 7

2. a. 34   b. 45   c. 61   d. 70   e. 46   f. 42
        x 4   x 5   x 6   x 8   x 5   x 7

3. a. 56   b. 67   c. 34   d. 90   e. 42   f. 66
        x 7   x 7   x 6   x 8   x 9   x 6

The 'multiplying by 10' machine

Professor Sharp invented a machine. It multiplies numbers by 10 very quickly. She drops in the number at one end and out comes the answer.

Can you discover how her machine works?

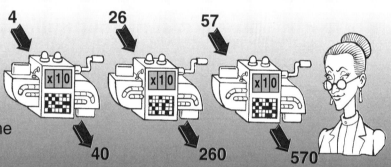

Can you multiply each of these numbers by 10?

4. a. 21   b. 34   c. 35   d. 67   e. 22   f. 65   g. 43   h. 75

5. a. 137   b. 288   c. 392   d. 430   e. 558   f. 673   g. 732   h. 845

6. A box holds 48 bars. How many bars are there in 10 boxes?

7. A tyre for a lorry costs €75. How much will it cost to buy 10 new tyres for the lorry?

8. If there are 10 classes in a school and 32 children in each class, how many children are there in the school?

9. If a lorry can carry 25 crates of fruit, how many crates of fruit can 10 lorries carry?

If you want to multiply a number by **20**, first drop it into Professor Sharp's machine and then multiply by 2.

```
      23
    x 20
```

23

```
So    230
      x 2
      460
```

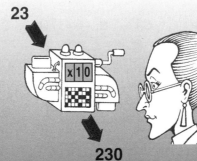

230

```
      23
    x 20
      460
```

How would you multiply by 30, 40 or 50?

1. a. 43   b. 34   c. 31   d. 41   e. 52   f. 73
      x 20   x 20   x 20   x 20   x 20   x 20

2. a. 24   b. 35   c. 72   d. 81   e. 92   f. 74
      x 30   x 30   x 30   x 40   x 40   x 40

3. a. 54   b. 76   c. 92   d. 63   e. 68   f. 95
      x 50   x 50   x 60   x 70   x 80   x 90

4. a. 113   b. 114   c. 118   d. 121   e. 117
      x 4   x 8   x 7   x 8   x 8

5. a. 247   b. 254   c. 238   d. 331   e. 335
      x 4   x 3   x 4   x 3   x 2

6. a. 293   b. 386   c. 475   d. 573   e. 698
      x 4   x 8   x 7   x 8   x 8

Example:
```
    1 2 8
    x ₁ ₅7
    8 9 6
```

1. a.   125   b.   162   c.   144   d.   183
    x   20   x   40   x   50   x   30

Example:
3 1 6
x ₁3 0
9,4 8 0

Example:

$$\begin{array}{r} 3\,1\,6 \\ \times \,{}_1 3\,0 \\ \hline 9,4\,8\,0 \end{array}$$

2. a.   234   b.   258   c.   267   d.   299
    x   40   x   30   x   30   x   20

3. a.   132   b.   142   c.   225   d.   331
    x   60   x   70   x   30   x   20

4. a.   156   b.   149   c.   304   d.   265
    x   20   x   40   x   30   x   30

5. **Multiply each of these numbers by 40:**

   a. 236   b. 246   c. 168   d. 157   e. 221

6. A box holds 27 packets of sweets. How many packets are there in 40 boxes?

7. A guard was on duty in a small town. One night he walked around the town 30 times and, as he did so, he checked each of the 13 shops. How many checks did he make altogether during his patrol?

8. A bakery supplies 20 shops with bread. How many loaves of bread does the bakery need to make if each shop orders 166 loaves?

9. The teacher was in a good mood and decided to buy an ice pop for each of his 28 pupils. How much did it cost him if an ice pop is 30c and he also bought one for himself?

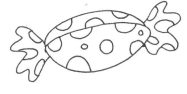

10. A deck of cards has 52 cards and 2 jokers. How many cards, including jokers, are there in 20 decks?

11. Dave gets 32 points every time he shops in a particular supermarket. He has shopped there every week for the past 30 weeks. He needs 1,000 points to get a radio. Has he got enough points yet?
How many more does he need?

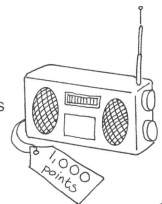

Peter sells the *Morning Echo* newspaper.
It costs 95c. One day he sold 63 newspapers.
How much money did he have at the end of the day?

We need to find 63 times 95c (63 x 95).
We could add 95 sixty-three times (95 + 95 + 95 + 95 + 95 + ... 63 times).
Is there an easier way?

Let's suppose Peter sold **60** newspapers in the morning and only **3** in the afternoon.

In the morning he took in   95   and in the afternoon   95
60 times 95:   x ₃ 60   3 times 95:   x ₁ 3
                             5700 cent   285 cent

Now we put our two answers together:

$$5700 + 285 = 5985 \text{ cent (or €59·85)}$$

This type of multiplication is called **long multiplication**. We write it like this:

	95
	x 63
Multiply 95 by 3	285
Multiply 95 by 60	5700
Add your two answers	5985

1. a.   34   b.   56   c.   31   d.   53   e.   61   f.   41
       x 12   x 14   x 15   x 19   x 16   x 17

2. a.   35   b.   44   c.   42   d.   67   e.   28   f.   35
       x 23   x 25   x 23   x 31   x 33   x 41

Just for fun!
When Noah said to the creatures on the Ark, "Go forth and multiply," the animals were delighted and they ran off. When they had all left he found two snakes in the corner crying. "What's wrong?" he asked. "We can't multiply," they replied, "we're adders."

1. A PE hall floor has 42 rows of tiles. If there are 24 tiles in each row, how many tiles cover the floor?

2. A jam factory makes 44 kilogrammes of jam every hour. How many kilogrammes will it produce in 24 hours?

3.
a. 45
   x 46

b. 67
   x 45

c. 88
   x 63

d. 73
   x 56

e. 91
   x 89

f. 82
   x 68

4.
a. 68
   x 72

b. 85
   x 35

c. 39
   x 41

d. 93
   x 19

e. 94
   x 27

f. 86
   x 35

5.
a. 31 x 123 = ☐

b. 42 x 224 = ☐

c. 25 x 139 = ☐

d. 35 x 226 = ☐

e. 56 x 144 = ☐

f. 54 x 105 = ☐

g. 26 x 309 = ☐

h. 21 x 274 = ☐

i. 36 x 190 = ☐

6. An aeroplane can carry 72 passengers. How many passengers can it carry in a month if it makes 62 flights during the month?

7. A hotel has 24 rooms. Each room has a vase that holds 16 flowers. How many fresh flowers must the manager order every morning?

8. A shirt has 10 buttons down the front and 2 on each sleeve. How many buttons must a shirt-maker order if he wishes to make 124 new shirts?

9. A dealer buys 36 items at 52c each and sells them at 98c each.
   a. How much does she spend buying the items?
   b. How much money will she have when she sells all the items?
   c. How much more money will she have at the end than at the start?

10. A train goes under 14 bridges when it travels from Sunny Valley to Windy Gap. How many times altogether does it go under a bridge if it goes from Sunny Valley to Windy Gap and back 22 times?

1.
a. (3 x 4) + 11 = ☐	b. (4 x 7) + 12 = ☐	c. (3 x 9) + 8 = ☐
d. (4 x 9) + 13 = ☐	e. (5 x 7) + 9 = ☐	f. (8 x 8) – 10 = ☐
g. (9 x 8) – 7 = ☐	h. (7 x 6) – 12 = ☐	i. (8 x 6) – 13 = ☐
j. (6 x 11) – 7 = ☐	k. 20 – (4 x 5) = ☐	l. 30 – (4 x 7) = ☐
m. 50 – (7 x 7) = ☐	n. 70 – (8 x 8) = ☐	o. 80 – (9 x 8) = ☐

2.
a. 40 x 30 = ☐	b. 50 x 60 = ☐	c. 40 x 20 = ☐
d. 80 x 90 = ☐	e. 70 x 30 = ☐	f. 40 x 50 = ☐

3.
a. 90 x 20 = ☐	b. 70 x 20 = ☐	c. 60 x 40 = ☐
d. 30 x 50 = ☐	e. 50 x 70 = ☐	f. 90 x 90 = ☐

A calculator makes long multiplication very easy. We want to find 37 x 45:

Press   **=**

You should find the answer 1,665 appearing instantly on your screen.

Estimate the answers. (Round to the nearest 10.)
Use your calculator to see how close you were.

4.
a. 57 x 87 = ☐	b. 56 x 63 = ☐	c. 65 x 54 = ☐
d. 76 x 36 = ☐	e. 57 x 78 = ☐	f. 79 x 81 = ☐
g. 75 x 11 = ☐	h. 38 x 52 = ☐	i. 28 x 43 = ☐

5.
a. 21 x 22 = ☐	b. 83 x 83 = ☐	c. 8 x 87 = ☐
d. 62 x 34 = ☐	e. 34 x 39 = ☐	f. 89 x 92 = ☐
g. 94 x 44 = ☐	h. 67 x 45 = ☐	i. 48 x 73 = ☐

6. A tiler can put up 38 tiles in an hour. She needs to put up 1,600 tiles and she estimated it would take her 43 hours. Would you agree with her estimate? Now use your calculator to see if she will get the job done in time.

As you can see the design is made from 10 stars and it points upwards. Can you choose 3 stars and reposition them so that the design points downwards?

Unit 7 – Division

You will need **Multilink Cubes (or counters)**.
Put 12 **Multilink Cubes** in front of you.
Divide them into sets of 4 as you see in the picture.
How many sets of 4 are there?
In maths we write 12 ÷ 4 = 3.

1. Now divide the 12 **Multilink Cubes** into sets of 3.
   How many sets are there?   Write 12 ÷ 3 = ☐

2. Divide the 12 **Multilink Cubes** into sets of 6.
   How many sets are there?   Write 12 ÷ 6 = ☐

3. Divide the 12 **Multilink Cubes** into sets of 2.
   How many sets are there?   Write 12 ÷ 2 = ☐

4. Put 20 **Multilink Cubes** in front of you.
   Divide them into sets of 5 as you see in the picture.
   How many sets of 5 are there?
   Now write a division sentence for this: ☐ ÷ 5 = ☐

5. Now divide the 20 **Multilink Cubes** into sets of 4.
   Write a division sentence to show this.

6. How many sets of 10 can you make from the 20 cubes?
   Write a division sentence.

7. How many sets of 2 can you make from the 20 cubes?
   Write a division sentence.

> **Remember!**
> The symbol ÷ means **divided by**, **in sets of** or **shared between**.

8. **Count out 24 Multilink Cubes. Divide them into groups of:**
   a. 6   b. 4   c. 12   d. 2   e. 8   f. 3
   Write a division sentence for each.

9. **Write each of these as a division sentence and find the answer.**
   a. A group of boys ate 35 sweets altogether.
       If they each ate 7 sweets, how many boys were there?

   b. A farmer looked into his field of sheep and counted 32 legs.
       How many sheep did he see?

   c. Paul has €45. He spends €5 every day. How long will his money last?

1.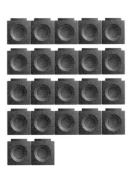

   Select 15 **Multilink Cubes**.
   Divide them into sets of 6 as you see in the picture.
   How many sets of 6 are there?
   In maths we write 15 ÷ 6 = 2 r 3.
   The letter **r** stands for **remainder** – what is left over.
   Divide the 15 **Multilink Cubes** into sets of 7.
   Is there a remainder? Write a division sentence.

2. Select 22 **Multilink Cubes**.
   Divide them into sets of 5 as you see in the picture.
   How many sets of 5 are there?
   Is there a remainder?
   Write a division sentence.
   Divide the 22 **Multilink Cubes** into sets of 8.
   Write a division sentence.

3. **Count out 18 Multilink Cubes. Divide them into groups of:**

   a. 6   b. 4   c. 12   d. 2   e. 8   f. 3

   Write a division sentence for each.

4. **Write each of these as a division sentence and find the answer.**

   a. If it takes 8 bars of chocolate to fill a box, how many **complete** boxes
       could I fill if I have 39 bars?

   b. If your holidays lasted for 40 days, how many **full**
       weeks would you have?

   c. Noel ordered 5 taxis to bring 22 people to a concert.
       Each taxi would only carry 4 people.
       How many people had to take the bus?

   d. A minibus can carry 9 passengers at most.
       How many minibuses would I need to bring 30
       people on a trip?

   e. Pat, Rita and Sean have 26 sweets altogether. If they share them equally,
       how many will each person get and how many will be left over?

   f. Terry had a €20 note. He changed it into 20 one euro coins and
       shared them with his two friends. How much did Terry get if he also
       got the remainder?

1.
a.	$12 \div 3 =$	
b.	$14 \div 2 =$	
c.	$21 \div 7 =$	
d.	$22 \div 11 =$	
e.	$24 \div 8 =$	
f.	$30 \div 10 =$	
g.	$28 \div 7 =$	
h.	$36 \div 6 =$	
i.	$32 \div 4 =$	

2.
a.	$63 \div 9 =$	
b.	$72 \div 8 =$	
c.	$81 \div 9 =$	
d.	$56 \div 8 =$	
e.	$60 \div 6 =$	
f.	$48 \div 8 =$	
g.	$33 \div 3 =$	
h.	$64 \div 8 =$	
i.	$49 \div 7 =$	

3.
a.	$24 \div$	$= 8$
b.	$25 \div$	$= 5$
c.	$36 \div$	$= 9$
d.	$56 \div$	$= 8$
e.	$49 \div$	$= 7$
f.	$63 \div$	$= 9$
g.	$72 \div$	$= 8$
h.	$81 \div$	$= 9$
i.	$90 \div$	$= 10$

4. A tray holds 6 eggs. How many trays can I fill if I have 48 eggs?

5.

An archer scored 27 points with 3 arrows. What did she score with each arrow if they each hit the same part of the target?

6. Katie had €35 in the post office and she decided to take it out. She asked the lady behind the counter to give her the money in €5 notes. How many €5 notes did she get?

7. How many times can I fill a watering can that holds 5 litres from a barrel that holds 45 litres?

8. How many 7kg bags of potatoes can I fill from a pile that weighs 50kg?

9. There are 23 people going to a game. How many minibuses do I need to order if a minibus can carry 8 passengers?

PUZZLE POWER

There are 20 socks in a drawer. Ten of them are blue and 10 are black. The room is pitch dark. What is the least number of socks that I need to take out to be certain of having: a. a matching pair? b. a blue pair?

1. a. 39 ÷ 3 = ☐   b. 48 ÷ 4 = ☐   c. 44 ÷ 2 = ☐   d. 88 ÷ 4 = ☐

2. a. 42 ÷ 3 = ☐   b. 56 ÷ 4 = ☐   c. 75 ÷ 5 = ☐   d. 98 ÷ 7 = ☐

3. a. 45 ÷ 3 = ☐   b. 84 ÷ 7 = ☐   c. 95 ÷ 5 = ☐   d. 68 ÷ 4 = ☐

4. How many €5 notes would I get for 65 one euro coins?

5. How many times can I take 6 from 84?

6. A deck of cards has 52 cards (excluding the 2 jokers).
   If I share all 52 cards between myself and my friend,
   how many will we each get?

Example:

$4 \overline{)9\,{}^{1}6}$ OR $4\overline{)9\,{}^{1}6}$
24 24

7. Four classes of 24 children go to the hall. They are told to break up into
   groups of 3. How many groups will there be?

8. a. 34 ÷ 3 = ☐   b. 29 ÷ 2 = ☐   c. 46 ÷ 4 = ☐   d. 57 ÷ 5 = ☐

9. a. 47 ÷ 9 = ☐   b. 66 ÷ 8 = ☐   c. 74 ÷ 5 = ☐   d. 98 ÷ 3 = ☐

10. a. 73 ÷ 6 = ☐   b. 99 ÷ 7 = ☐   c. 99 ÷ 8 = ☐   d. 99 ÷ 4 = ☐

11. a. 54 ÷ 4 = ☐   b. 88 ÷ 7 = ☐   c. 76 ÷ 5 = ☐   d. 84 ÷ 5 = ☐

12. I need 70 blocks to build a patio. The shop only sells blocks
    in packs of 9. How many packs do I need to buy?

13. A young apple tree normally yields around 8 apples.
    A gardener had a crop of 41 apples.
    All his trees are young.
    How many trees do you think he owns?

14. A red ball in snooker scores 1 point and
    a black ball scores 7 points. Ken put a
    red ball into a pocket, then a black ball,
    then a red, then a black and so on.
    He scored 97 points before he missed.
    How many red balls did he sink?

Example:

675 ÷ 5

```
      1 3 5                    5 │ 6 ¹7 ²5
5 │ 6 ¹7 ²5       OR              1 3 5
```

1. a. 844 ÷ 4 = ☐   b. 246 ÷ 2 = ☐   c. 936 ÷ 3 = ☐

2. a. 144 ÷ 3 = ☐   b. 165 ÷ 5 = ☐   c. 318 ÷ 2 = ☐

3. a. 243 ÷ 9 = ☐   b. 352 ÷ 8 = ☐   c. 616 ÷ 7 = ☐

4. a. 456 ÷ 6 = ☐   b. 837 ÷ 9 = ☐   c. 987 ÷ 7 = ☐

Don't forget your zero.

Example:

832 ÷ 4

```
        2 0 8                  4 │ 8 3 ³2
4 │ 8 3 ³2         OR              2 0 8
```

5. a. 525 ÷ 5 = ☐   b. 642 ÷ 6 = ☐   c. 918 ÷ 9 = ☐

6. a. 906 ÷ 3 = ☐   b. 728 ÷ 7 = ☐   c. 936 ÷ 9 = ☐

7. a. 202 ÷ 5 = ☐   b. 183 ÷ 6 = ☐   c. 424 ÷ 7 = ☐

8.  A farmer has 135 cows and 5 fields. How many cows will she put in each field if she puts the same number of cows in each field?

9. An electric lawnmower costs 4 times as much as a push mower.
   If the electric mower costs €196, find the cost of:
   a. a push mower
   b. a push mower and an electric mower.

10.  A supermarket decided one day to give a free bunch of flowers to every 7th customer. How many bunches were needed if there were 455 customers?

11. A book costs 8 times as much as a copybook. If the book costs €3·84 (384c) how much will I pay for a book and a copybook?

12. A factory makes 126 cars in 3 days.
    How many cars will it make in 5 days?

1. A garage is giving free sweets to every 5th customer: so the 5th customer, the 10th customer and so on get free sweets. If you were customer number 273, would you be one of the lucky ones?

2. John was visited by 5 of his friends. He counted his sweets and found that he had 159 sweets. He shared them equally. How many did John give himself if he took his share **and** whatever was left over?

3. If a CD costs €9, how many can I buy for €110?

4. If an orange costs 8c, how much will I have left over if I buy as many oranges as I can for €1? (Hint: Change €1 to 100c.)

5. There are 32 children in a class. The teacher wishes to divide the class into equal groups. In how many different ways can she do it? (There must be at least 2 children in each group.)

6. There are 146 children in a school. The Principal wants to divide the children into 7 groups. How will she do it if she wants to make the groups as equal in size as possible?

■ If a number is even, there is no remainder when you divide by 2.

■ Add up the digits of a number.
If 3 goes into your answer evenly then 3 goes into the number itself evenly.

Example:	**144 ÷ 3**	Is there a remainder?
	1 + 4 + 4 = 9	3 goes into 9 evenly, so it will also go into 144 evenly.

■ If a number ends in 0 or 5, then 5 will go into it evenly.

■ If a number ends in 0, then 10 will go into it evenly.

---

7. **Tick (just by looking) if there is a remainder in each of these:**

a. 516 ÷ 2 = ☐   b. 635 ÷ 3 = ☐   c. 444 ÷ 2 = ☐

d. 452 ÷ 3 = ☐   e. 553 ÷ 3 = ☐   f. 356 ÷ 5 = ☐

g. 663 ÷ 5 = ☐   h. 900 ÷ 10 = ☐   i. 852 ÷ 10 = ☐

j. 132 ÷ 10 = ☐   k. 560 ÷ 10 = ☐   l. 802 ÷ 2 = ☐

To enter 460 ÷ 5 on your calculator:

Press   =

Does a calculator give you remainders?

Using your calculator, find the answer to each of these questions then multiply your answer by the smaller number (the divisor). What do you notice?

1. a. 648 ÷ 9 = ☐   b. 558 ÷ 9 = ☐   c. 445 ÷ 5 = ☐

2. a. 235 ÷ 5 = ☐   b. 976 ÷ 2 = ☐   c. 945 ÷ 5 = ☐

3. a. 8,748 ÷ 6 = ☐   b. 1,808 ÷ 4 = ☐   c. 1,393 ÷ 7 = ☐

PUZZLE POWER

The teacher was explaining in class one day that a **polygon** is a shape like a triangle or hexagon. "Can anyone in the class think of another example of a polygon?" she asked. Alfie, who had been half asleep at the back of the class, put his hand up and said...

To decode what Alfie said, work out the answers to these questions. Then wherever you see your answer in the code-grid, put in whichever letter is beside the question. Your answer might appear more than once.

For example:

N   432 ÷ 9 = 48   The answer is 48. So write **N** underneath any 48.

D   594 ÷ 6 = ☐   U   427 ÷ 7 = ☐   E   445 ÷ 5 = ☐

G   264 ÷ 8 = ☐   F   243 ÷ 9 = ☐   S   865 ÷ 5 = ☐

H   882 ÷ 9 = ☐   T   315 ÷ 7 = ☐   O   684 ÷ 9 = ☐

Y   348 ÷ 4 = ☐   I   879 ÷ 3 = ☐   L   932 ÷ 4 = ☐

A   882 ÷ 6 = ☐   P   833 ÷ 7 = ☐   R   392 ÷ 7 = ☐

W   948 ÷ 6 = ☐

147		119	76	233	87	33	76	48		293	173		147
A		P	O	L	Y	G	O	N		I	S		A

119	147	56	56	76	45		158	98	76		27	233	89	158
P	A	R	R	O	T		W	H	O		F	L	E	W

76	61	45		45	98	89		158	293	48	99	76	158
O	U	I		T	H	E		W	I	N	D	O	W

Poor Cinderella. She was warned: "Don't stay at the ball after midnight or you'll be sorry." But she forgot to keep an eye on the time and when midnight came, her beautiful clothes turned into rags. But that's not the full story. Cinderella **was** watching the time very closely indeed, but in those days there were no fancy clocks such as the ones we have nowadays. The Prince was burning special candles which had little markings down the side that were supposed to tell the time. Of course, these weren't very accurate, as Cinderella knows all too well.

1. Name two other ways people told the time long ago before modern clocks were invented. Why don't people use these methods nowadays?

2. **What time does each clock face show?**

   a.  b.  c.  d.

3. **Look again at each of the clock faces. What time will the clock show:**

   a. $\frac{1}{2}$ an hour later   b. $\frac{3}{4}$ of an hour later   c. $1\frac{1}{4}$ hours later?

4. a. 1 hr 20 mins = _____ mins   b. 2 hrs 35 mins = _____ mins

5. a. 100 mins = _____ hr _____ mins   b. 110 mins = _____ hr _____ mins

6. a. 55 mins + 45 mins = _____ hr _____ mins

   b. 2 hours – 35 mins = _____ hr _____ mins

7. Write $\frac{1}{4}$ past 6 as you would see it on a video recorder.

8. How many minutes are there between 2:45 and 3:30?

a.    b. 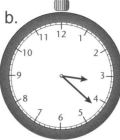   c. 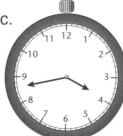   d.

Clock a: The time shown here is 10 minutes past 3.
Clock b: Here the big hand is between 4 and 5. It is 22 minutes past 3.
Clock c: Here the big hand is between 8 and 9. It is 17 minutes to 4.
Clock d: Here the big hand is between 11 and 12. It is 1 minute to 4.

1. Write the time each clock shows:

a.    b.    c.    d.

_____   _____   _____   _____

e.    f.    g.    h.

_____   _____   _____   _____

P 2. **Draw the hands on blank clock faces to show these times:**

    a. 20 past 6   b. 9 minutes past 4   c. 29 minutes past 2
    d. half past 9   e. 11 minutes to 1   f. 1 minute past 8
    g. quarter to 10   h. 3 minutes past 7   i. 28 minutes to 11

3. Write how many minutes there are between:

    a. 10 past 3 and $\frac{1}{2}$ past 3   b. 20 to 4 and 24 mins past 4
    c. 25 past 5 and 10 to 6   d. 12 mins to 12 and 25 past 12
    e. 16 mins past 8 and $\frac{1}{4}$ to 9   f. 23 mins to 10 and $\frac{1}{2}$ past 10

Digital time
5 past 3 = 3:05
$\frac{1}{4}$ past 3 = 3:15
20 past 3 = 3:20
20 to 4 = 3:40
$\frac{1}{4}$ to 4 = 3:45

1. **Change these to digital form:**
   a. 20 past 6
   b. quarter past 8
   c. 25 past 11
   d. 6 minutes past 3
   e. 9 minutes past 8
   f. 13 minutes past 2
   g. 5 minutes to 12
   h. 8 minutes to 1
   i. 1 minute to 5
   j. 3 minutes to 3
   k. 29 minutes to 4
   l. 19 minutes to 6

2. **Write each of these in a different way. Example 2:05 = 5 past 2.**
   a. 2:20
   b. 7:15
   c. 2:55
   d. 1:35
   e. 10:01
   f. 8:30
   g. 6:45
   h. 4:35
   i. 3:13
   j. 10:32
   k. 12:05
   l. 12:50
   m. 9:55
   n. 6:27
   o. 11:59

3. **Write how many minutes there are between:**
   a. 2:20 and 2:28
   b. 3:35 and 3:55
   c. 4:40 and 5:22
   d. 4:05 and 4:30
   e. 10:40 and 11:00
   f. 6:35 and 7:12
   g. 6:00 and 6:45
   h. 12:35 and 1:05
   i. 8:45 and 9:28

3:00	Kids TV
3:20	Cartoons
3:45	Kids Pet Vet
4:00	Son of Tarzan
4:30	Enid Blyton Adventures
5:05	Tales of Sorcery
5:35	Detective Dick
6:00	News
6:15	Brooke Street
6:45	The Chart Show
7:00	Blackboard Jungle

4. **Examine the TV guide and answer the questions based on it.**
   a. How long does the cartoon programme last?
   b. Which programme starts at 5 past 5?
   c. Which programme ends at 6:45?
   d. Which programme lasts longest?
   e. Which three programmes last for a quarter of an hour each?
   f. Tim watched *Son of Tarzan* and *The Chart Show*. How long did he spend watching TV?
   g. If every programme was running 12 minutes late, at what time would each programme start?

5. A clock shows a time of 3:05. It is 15 minutes fast. What is the actual time?

6. Mark started to read at 7:40 and he read for 55 minutes. At what time did he stop reading?

7. A film starts at 8:11. If it is now 7 minutes to 8 how long will it be before the film begins?

58

1. **Write these as hours and minutes.**
   Example: 90 minutes = 1 hour 30 minutes.

a. 70 mins	b. 110 mins	c. 115 mins	d. 119 mins
80 mins	65 mins	73 mins	99 mins
100 mins	105 mins	107 mins	120 mins

2. **Write these as minutes.**
   Example: 2 hours 21 mins = (2 x 60) + 21 = 141 mins.
   a. 1 hr 15 mins   b. 1 hr 35 mins   c. 1 hr 43 mins
   d. 2 hrs 11 mins   e. 2 hrs 23 mins   f. 2 hrs 55 mins
   g. 3 hrs 48 mins   h. 4 hrs 14 mins   i. 5 hrs 5 mins

   Adding hours and minutes

   Add the hours and minutes separately. If you have
   60 minutes or more, change them to hours and minutes.

hrs	mins
2	50
+ 3	58
5	108 ———→ 1 hr 48 mins

   So my answer is 6 hours 48 minutes.

3.
a. **hrs mins**	b. **hrs mins**	c. **hrs mins**	d. **hrs mins**	e. **hrs mins**
2 40	3 35	4 56	5 48	8 59
+ 3 50	+ 4 25	+ 3 24	+ 7 48	+ 6 46

4. **Add these the same way:**
   a. 2 hrs 23 mins + 2 hrs 35 mins
   b. 7 hrs 25 mins + 3 hrs 52 mins
   c. 2 hrs 12 mins + 3 hrs 48 mins

   Just for fun!
   "How many seconds in a year?" asked Jim.
   "31,536,000," replied Colm after a lot of calculating.
   "Not at all," said Jim, "Only 12: Second of January, second of February, second of March..."

5.
a. **hrs mins**	b. **hrs mins**	c. **hrs mins**
2 30	4 50	4 42
3 50	1 40	3 52
+ 1 20	+ 1 40	+ 1 38

If you need to rename, remember to change the hour to 60 minutes.			
hrs	**mins**	**hrs**	**mins**
4	28	4³	88
− 1	52	− 1	52
		2	36

1. **Subtract these:**

a. **hrs mins**	b. **hrs mins**	c. **hrs mins**	d. **hrs mins**	e. **hrs mins**
5 50	4 40	6 56	7 23	6 12
− 2 23	− 1 50	− 4 49	− 4 36	− 1 25

2. **Subtract these in the same way:**

   a. 3 hrs 50 mins − 1 hr 15 mins
   b. 8 hrs 4 mins − 3 hrs 26 mins
   c. 7 hrs 47 mins − 2 hrs 27 mins
   d. 6 hrs 16 mins − 1 hr 25 mins
   e. 7 hrs 25 mins − 3 hrs 7 mins
   f. 9 hrs 12 mins − 7 hrs 58 mins

3. Mr Murphy usually works for 6 hours 30 minutes every day.
   Last Tuesday he was not feeling well and he went home
   2 hours 45 minutes early. How long did he spend at work that day?

4. Last week Michelle spent 14 hours 30 minutes training.
   Claire was also training. She spent 2 hours 55 minutes
   less than Michelle training. For how long did Claire train?

5. How many times each day does a stopped clock
   show the right time?

6.
   A surgeon finished an operation at 2:35.
   She took a break and started another operation at 4:10.
   How long was her break?

PUZZLE POWER

If it takes me 1 minute to saw through a plank of wood,
how long will it take me to divide a plank of wood into
12 pieces? Draw a picture to show your answer.

A.M. AND P.M.

> Times between midnight and noon are written as **a.m.**
> Times between noon and midnight are written as **p.m.**

1. **Write these using a.m. or p.m. Answer in digital time.**
   Example: 20 past 3 in the afternoon is 3:20 p.m.

   a. 6 o'clock in the morning
   b. 10 o'clock at night
   c. 7:45 in the evening
   d. Half past 3 when you're asleep

2. **Write what you are usually doing at each of these times:**
   a. 5:00 a.m.   b. 4:00 p.m.   c. 7:30 p.m.   d. 12:30 p.m.   e. 9:50 a.m.

THE CALENDAR

> 1 year = 12 months = 52 weeks = 365 days
> (366 in a leap year)

Sun	Mon	Tue	Wed	Thur	Fri	Sat
		1	2	3	4	5
6	7	8	9	10	11	12
13	14	15	16	17	18	19
20	21	22	23	24	25	26
27	28	29	30	31		

3. **This calendar page shows the month of March.**
   Write the day on which each of these dates in March falls:
   a. 1st   b. 5th   c. 9th   d. 14th   e. 15th   f. 23rd

4. On what day does the 1st of April fall?

5. On what day does the 28th of February fall if the year is not a leap year?

6. On what day does the 28th of February fall if the year is a leap year?

7. Why do you think the 17th of March is underlined?

8. The clock usually 'goes forward' in March.
   Can you explain what that means?

1. **This timetable shows the times of two trains travelling from Dublin to Galway.**

	Special	Express
Dublin	1:00 p.m.	7:00 p.m.
Kildare	1:30 p.m.	7:25 p.m.
Athlone	2:30 p.m.	8:15 p.m.
Athenry	3:30 p.m.	9:05 p.m.
Galway	4:00 p.m.	9:30 p.m.

a. How long does the Special take to get from Dublin to Athlone?
b. How long does the Express take to get from Kildare to Athenry?
c. How many minutes would you save by taking the Express from Athlone to Galway instead of the Special?

2. **This timetable shows the times of two buses travelling from Limerick to Rosslare.**

	Rapid-Bus	Swift-Bus
Limerick	4:00 p.m.	7:20 p.m.
Cahir	5:10 p.m.	——
Clonmel	5:30 p.m.	——
Waterford	6:15 p.m.	9:20 p.m.
Rosslare	7:10 p.m.	10:10 p.m.

a. The Swift-Bus has no times shown for Cahir or Clonmel even though it passes through both these towns. Why do you think this is so?
b. Which bus takes less time travelling from Limerick to Rosslare?
c. A man got on the Rapid-Bus in Cahir and got off at Waterford. How long did his journey take?
d. One day the Rapid-Bus got a puncture and was delayed in Cahir for 35 minutes.
   At what time did it reach: a. Clonmel? b. Waterford? c. Rosslare?

ACTIVITIES!

Hold out one of your wrists. Using two fingers of your other hand feel for your pulse. Count how many times it beats in one minute. Do the same again immediately after PE. What do you notice?

Unit 9 – Money

1. **Find the price of each of the following items:**

   a. litre of milk   b. this maths book   c. loaf of bread

   d. blue biro   e. bottle of lemonade   f. stamp to post a letter

   g. callcard   h. 88 page copy   i. a piece of cheese

2. **Compare your answers with a partner's.**

   Which ones are different from your partner's?

   How much is there in the difference?

   Make a chart like this:

Items with same price		Items with different prices		
Item	Price	Item	My price	Friend's price
Stamp	_____ cent	Piece of cheese	_____ cent	_____ cent

3. Two items might have different prices because they were bought in different shops.

   Can you think of any other reasons why two items might have different prices?

4.
   a. €3·45 = ☐ c

   b. €6·78 = ☐ c

   c. €3·51 = ☐ c

   d. €5·55 = ☐ c

   e. €4·03 = ☐ c

5.
   a. €0·72 = ☐ c

   b. €0·60 = ☐ c

   c. €0·15 = ☐ c

   d. €0·03 = ☐ c

   e. €0·09 = ☐ c

6.
   a. 381c = € ☐

   b. 654c = € ☐

   c. 987c = € ☐

   d. 125c = € ☐

   e. 48c = € ☐

> **3 items @ 5c** means that each of the items costs 5c.

7. **Write how much change (if any) I will get from €1·00 if I buy:**

   a. 6 items @ 10c   b. 5 items @ 20c   c. 4 items @ 20c

   d. 5 items @ 11c   e. 6 items @ 8c   f. 9 items @ 9c

   g. 4 items @ 21c   h. 7 items @ 9c   i. 6 items @ 15c

1. Write the **smallest number** of coins you could use to make the following.
   (Example: 6c=5c+1c)

   a. 7c   b. 13c   c. 38c   d. 63c   e. 99c
   f. €1·05   g. €2·77   h. €4·99   i. €2·44   j. 75c

2. Write the **smallest number** of coins you would get as change from €1,
   if you spent:

   a. 79c   b. 97c   c. 89c   d. 70c   e. 51c
   f. 48c   g. 31c   h. 3c   i. 14c   j. 63c

3. Write which coins would be best given as change from €5
   if you spent:

   a. €4·96   b. €4·91   c. €4·32   d. €4·01   e. €3·85
   f. €1·11   g. €1·02   h. €2·82   i. €1·75   j. €3·09

4. How many different ways can you make up 15c using coins?

5. **Answer these questions about the sale shown above.**

   a. By how much is each item reduced in the sale?

   b. Which item has:
      i. the greatest reduction?
      ii. the smallest reduction?

   c. If you bought every item at its sale price, how much
      would you save altogether?

   d. What is the greatest number of items you could buy for €100?
      (You may only buy one of each item.)

   e. Name two occasions when a shop might hold a sale.

	€
€4·56 + €3 + 76c	4 · 56
Be careful to keep the decimal points beneath one another.	3 · 00 ←
Don't forget your zeros. ——————————→	+ 0 · 76
	8 · 32

1. a. €4·56 + €3·58 + €2·55 = € ☐   b. €7·65 + €3·56 + €4·61 = € ☐

2. a. €4·02 + €6·78 + 67c = € ☐   b. 34c + €2 + €1·15 = € ☐

3. a. €2·34 + 13c + 3c = € ☐   b. €4 + 11c + 1c = € ☐

4. What is my shopping bill if I buy bread (€0·98), milk (€0·72) and cheese (€1·13)?

5. What will I pay for a bunch of daffodils (€1·99), a bunch of carnations (€2·99) and a bunch of irises (€3·99)?

6.  Mr Frosty, the polar bear in the zoo, is sick. How much does the keeper have to pay if the vet's bill is €37·50 and the medicine is €29·88?

7. A woman's yearly tax bill comes to €5,648. She also has a car loan which costs her €1,566 a year. What is the cost of paying both these bills?

8. Mr Smith's phone bill is €67·89, his electricity bill is €58·01 and his gas bill is €44·44. What is the total cost of the 3 bills?

9. Calculate the cost of Ernie's schoolbooks if he buys an English book (€6·67), an Irish book (€5·59), a maths book (€5·13) and a history book (€4).

10. A woman wants to fly to Australia. The travel agent tells her she must pay for five separate flights:
Shannon – Dublin (€39)
Dublin – London (€67)
London – Kuwait (€367)
Kuwait – Singapore (€345)
Singapore – Sydney (€185)
What is her total bill?

1. a. €2·45 – €1·24 = € ☐
    b. €8·61 – €7·70 = € ☐
    c. €4·95 – €2·67 = € ☐
    d. €5 – 56c = € ☐

2. a. €3·68 – €1·94 = € ☐
    b. €9·23 – €7·66 = € ☐
    c. (€5 – €4·56) + €2·33 = € ☐
    d. (€10 – €4·88) – €2·33 = € ☐

3. **What is my change when I buy the following?**
    a. a book for €3·82 if I pay with a €5 note
    b. a CD for €8·99 if I pay with a €10 note
    c. a blouse for €16·75 if I pay with a €20 note
    d. a pair of shoes for €27·95 if I pay with a €50 note

4. Bill pays €695 for a computer and €212·84 for a printer. What change will he get from €1,000?

5. Uncle Ned gets his windows cleaned (€4·50), his car washed (€3·60) and his grass mowed (€2·75). What change will he get from €20 if he also gives each of the three workers a €1·00 tip?

6. Auntie Margaret treated her family to Sunday lunch. What was her change from €50 if her lunch cost €5·95, Uncle John's cost €5·50, Monica's cost €4·50, Eric's cost €4·20 and they also had a bottle of wine costing €9·90?

7. Mick bought a second-hand car for €2,368. He spent €235·50 repairing and painting it. He then sold it for €2,750. Did he make a profit and, if so, how much?

PUZZLE POWER

A book and a pen cost €2·10. If the book costs €2·00 **more** than the pen, how much is the pen?

Did You Know?
The euro symbol was inspired by the Greek letter Epsilon. The letter E is the first letter of the word Europe.

Example:

€3·40
x   4
─────
€13·60

1. a. €4·20   b. €3·50   c. €2·28   d. €1·99   e. €2·99   f. €1·38
       x   4   x   5   x   7   x   9   x   4   x   5
    _____   _____   _____   _____   _____   _____

2. **How much will I pay if I buy:**
   a. 5 pairs of socks @ 99c a pair?
   b. 6 bunches of flowers @ €1·99 per bunch?
   c. 4 tickets for the cinema @ €3·95 each?
   d. 12 bottles of wine @ €5·95 per bottle?

3. If you were planning a birthday party for yourself and 5 friends, what would be the total cost:
   Bowling @ €2·60 per person and meal @ €4·25 per person?

4. A boat trip costs €2·50 per adult and €1·25 per child.
   What would 2 adults and 3 children have to pay?

5. A bank ordered 4 computers costing €780 each. What was the total cost if there was also a delivery and assembly charge of €12 per computer?

6. Sheila took 9 piano lessons and 8 swimming classes. The piano lessons were €2·20 each and the swimming classes were €1·80 each. She had a voucher for €10 towards the swimming classes. How much money did she have to pay?

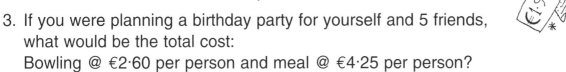

PUZZLE POWER

You have 20 coins totalling €1·25.
All of the coins are either 10c coins or 5c coins.
How many of each do you have?

1. a.   €

   4 | €5·56   b.   5 | €5·65   c.   3 | €7·11   d.   2 | €4·56   e.   9 | €4·41

2. a. €3·43 ÷ 7 = € ☐   b. €9·54 ÷ 6 = € ☐   c. €7·74 ÷ 9 = € ☐

   d. €7·85 ÷ 5 = € ☐   e. €7·56 ÷ 3 = € ☐   f. €8·16 ÷ 8 = € ☐

3. **Find the cost of 1 if:**
   a. 4 towels cost €4·96
   b. 3 books cost €7·92
   c. 7 plants cost €8·12
   d. 9 bars cost €4·68

4. **Find the cost of 2 if:**
   a. 3 pencils cost 21c
   b. 5 batteries cost €4·35
   c. 6 T-shirts cost €13·74
   d. 9 comics cost €5·67

PUZZLE POWER

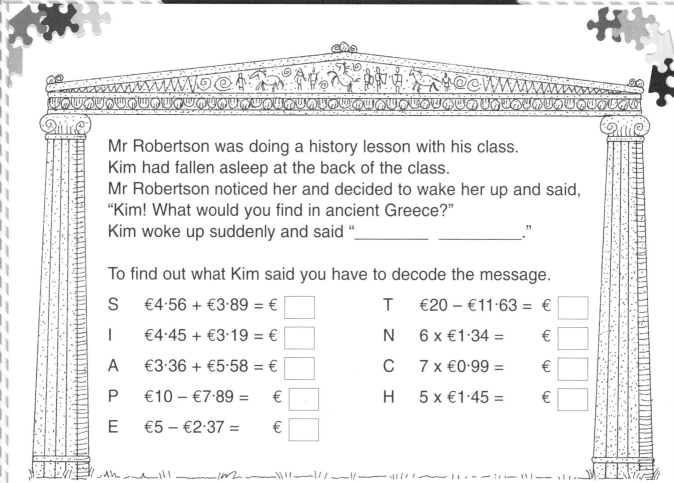

Mr Robertson was doing a history lesson with his class.
Kim had fallen asleep at the back of the class.
Mr Robertson noticed her and decided to wake her up and said,
"Kim! What would you find in ancient Greece?"
Kim woke up suddenly and said "_____ _____."

To find out what Kim said you have to decode the message.

S   €4·56 + €3·89 = € ☐   T   €20 − €11·63 = € ☐

I   €4·45 + €3·19 = € ☐   N   6 x €1·34 =   € ☐

A   €3·36 + €5·58 = € ☐   C   7 x €0·99 =   € ☐

P   €10 − €7·89 =   € ☐   H   5 x €1·45 =   € ☐

E   €5 − €2·37 =   € ☐

€8·94	€8·04	€6·93	€7·64	€2·63	€8·04	€8·37

€6·93	€7·25	€7·64	€2·11	€8·45

1. If you put your money into a post office or bank, you open an **account**. Write three reasons why it is a good idea to have a savings account.

2. A cheque saves us from carrying around lots of money. Name 3 things for which someone might write a cheque.

3. What happens if a person writes a cheque but has no money in his or her bank account?

> Many people use a **Laser** card to pay for their weekly shopping. The shopkeeper swipes the card and the money is taken from the customer's bank account and put into the shopkeeper's account.
>
> A **credit card** allows you to buy something now and to pay for it in a few weeks time. Many people use a credit card when buying things over the Internet.

INTERNET SHOPPING

Can they afford it?

4. Audrey has €20 to spend. She has a book (€4·40), a necklace (€6·80) and a video (€8·90) in her shopping basket.

5. Dermot has €100 to spend. He has a set of screwdrivers (€19·99), an electric drill €44·99) and an extension lead (€14·99) in his trolley.

6. Brian has €500. He has ordered a radio (€14·99), a TV (€299·99) and a new set of speakers (€169·99).

7. Deirdre has €1,000. She is buying a PC (€685), a printer (€135·50) and a digital camera (€159·49) with a €10 delivery charge.

"COUNT YOUR MONEY" SPEED TEST

You have 60 seconds! How much is in each of the 5 boxes?

8.  €_____

9.  €_____

10. 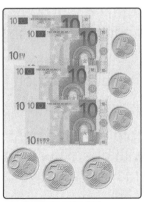 €_____

11.  €_____

12. €_____

1. **Write the correct name beside each shape. Choose from the following:**
   circle, rectangle, hexagon, triangle, square, oval, semicircle

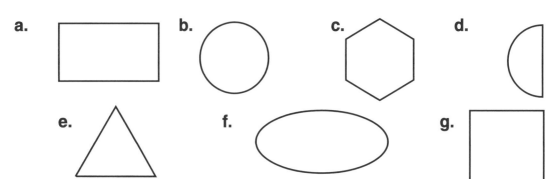

a.   b.   c.   d.

e.   f.   g.

There are different types of triangle.

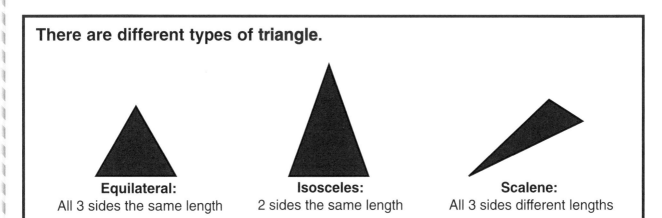

Equilateral:
All 3 sides the same length

Isosceles:
2 sides the same length

Scalene:
All 3 sides different lengths

---

2. On a blank piece of paper draw lots of each type of triangle.
   Try to draw a triangle with 2 sides that are parallel.
   Is it possible?

3. Draw a square. Draw a line that divides the square into
   2 equal triangles. Now draw a rectangle. Draw a line that
   divides the rectangle into two equal triangles. This line is called
   a diagonal.

4. Divide a square into 4 equal triangles by drawing 2 diagonals.
   Now divide a rectangle into 4 triangles by
   drawing 2 diagonals.

P 5. Can you make a regular hexagon from 6 equilateral triangles?

6. Are the angles of an equilateral triangle acute or obtuse?

7. Now draw a triangle with one right angle and two acute angles.
   Draw a triangle with one obtuse angle and two acute angles.
   Can you draw a triangle with two obtuse angles and
   one acute angle?

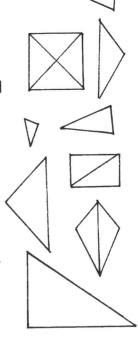

If we take a rectangle like this . . . . and push it out of shape like this

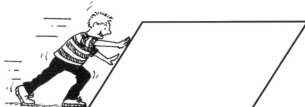

it becomes a parallelogram.

1. Use a ruler and set square to draw some parallelograms.

2. How many sides has a parallelogram?

3. How many **sets** of parallel lines has a parallelogram?

4. How many sides has a rectangle?

5. How many **sets** of parallel lines has a rectangle?

6. Did you get the same answers to questions 4 and 5 as you did to questions 2 and 3?

7. A rectangle is really a special type of parallelogram. What makes a rectangle special?

8. **True or false?**
   a. A rectangle never has perpendicular sides.
   b. A parallelogram sometimes has perpendicular sides.
   c. Every rectangle is a parallelogram.

9. **Into what shapes do you divide a parallelogram if you draw:**
   a. one diagonal?   b. both diagonals?

PUZZLE POWER

How many triangles can you see in each of these drawings?

a.   b.

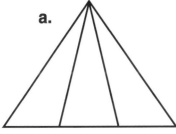

If we take a square like this . . . . and push it out of shape like this

it becomes
a **rhombus**

All 4 sides of a **rhombus** are the same length.

1. a. How many sides has a rhombus?
   b. How many sides has a square?

2. a. How many **sets** of parallel sides has a rhombus?
   b. How many **sets** of parallel sides has a square?

3. a. Is a rhombus a type of parallelogram?
   b. Is every parallelogram a rhombus?

4. What makes a rhombus a special type of parallelogram?

5. **Into what shapes do you divide a rhombus if you draw:**
   a. one diagonal?   b. both diagonals?

THE PENTAGON AND THE OCTAGON

A   B    C   D

Any shape with **5 sides** is called a **pentagon**. Shape **A** is a **regular pentagon** because the sides are **equal in length** and because the **angles are equal**.

6. Draw some pentagons.

7. How many angles has a regular pentagon?

8. Is each angle acute or obtuse?

9. Draw some octagons.

10. How many angles has a regular octagon?

11. Is each angle acute or obtuse?

12. How many sets of parallel lines has a regular octagon?

The Octagon

A 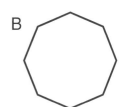 B

A shape with **8 sides** is an **octagon**. Shape A is an **octagon**. Shape B is a **regular octagon**.

1. How many **sides** and how many **angles** has each of the following shapes?
   How many **diagonals** could you draw?
   Name one place in the world around you where you might
   see the shape. Draw a chart like this:

Shape	Sides	Angles	Diagonals	Where you might see one
Square				
Rectangle				
Triangle				
Parallelogram				
Rhombus				
Pentagon				
Hexagon				
Octagon				

Say whether each of these statements is true or false:

2.   a.   A square is a rectangle.
    b.   The opposite sides of an octagon are parallel.
    c.   Bees make honey in hexagonal cells.
    d.   A set square is triangular in shape.
    e.   A parallelogram always has 4 right angles.
    f.   A parallelogram sometimes has 4 right angles.
    g.   A regular octagon has 4 sets of parallel lines.

PUZZLE POWER

P On a sheet of squared paper, see how many different
shapes you can make using 4 squares.
Each square must be connected to at least one other square.
Squares connected like this do not count: ⟶

> Shapes that fit together without leaving gaps or overlapping are said to **tessellate**.

1. Have you any tiles in your home or school? What shape are they?

2. **Look at each of the patterns. Colour in the shapes that tessellate.**

   a. **Rectangles**

   b. **Octagons**

   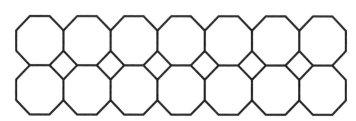

   c. **Pentagons**

   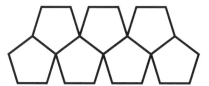

   d. **Equilateral Triangles**

   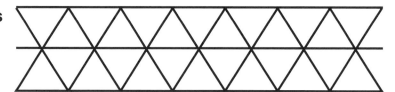

   e. **Circles**

   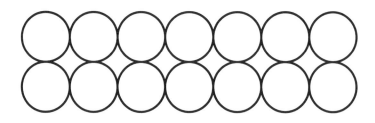

   f. **Ovals**

   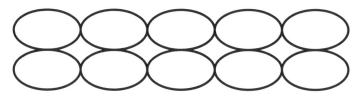

g. **Parallelograms**

h. **Hexagons**

3. Make some tessellating patterns of your own using suitable shapes.
   Colour some of the shapes to make an interesting design.

PUZZLE POWER

4. Use **Multilink Cubes** to make 10 copies of shape **a**. See if it tessellates.
   Now do the same for shapes **b**, **c** and **d**.

a.    b. 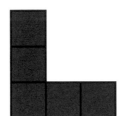   c.    d.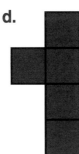

5. Make other designs using 4 or 5 **Multilink Cubes** and see if they tessellate.

1. **Double** each of these numbers:
   a. 5 b. 8 c. 11 d. 15 e. 21 f. 28
   g. 35 h. 37 i. 42 j. 54 k. 93 l. 67

2. Find **half** of each of these numbers:
   a. 16 b. 22 c. 28 d. 42 e. 50 f. 60
   g. 64 h. 68 i. 70 j. 82 k. 92 l. 56

3. A small theatre has 7 rows of seats. If there are 8 seats in each row, how many seats are in the theatre altogether if there are also 2 seats for VIPs?

4.  If I share 72 sweets equally among 8 people, how many will each person receive?

5. Which is longer: 1 hour 41 minutes or 99 minutes?

6. How many minutes from 2:20 p.m. to 3:12 p.m.?

7. Sheila usually works for 3 hours every afternoon. Yesterday she went home 17 minutes early. For how many hours and minutes did she work yesterday afternoon?

8. 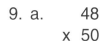 A bus that usually leaves at 11:55 a.m. was delayed for 12 minutes. At what time did it set out?

9. a. 48
      x 50
   b. 85
      x 30
   c. 96
      x 40
   d. 87
      x 60
   e. 69
      x 80
   f. 94
      x 70

10. A boy has done 24 rows of knitting. There are 42 stitches in each row. How many stitches has he done?

11. A roof has 18 rows of slates. There are 32 slates in each row. Work out the cost of buying new slates for the roof if slates cost €3 each.

12. Add 2 hours 45 minutes, 2 hours 36 minutes and 2 hours 23 minutes.

13. a. $536 \div 2 =$ ☐
    b. $639 \div 3 =$ ☐
    c. $736 \div 4 =$ ☐
    d. $135 \div 5 =$ ☐
    e. $732 \div 6 =$ ☐
    f. $423 \div 9 =$ ☐

1. An apple costs 9c. How much will I have left over if I buy as many apples as I can for €2?

2. A book costs 4 times as much as a marker. If the marker costs 65c, how much change will I get from €5 if I buy a book and a marker?

3. Michael bought an old bicycle for €35. He bought paint (€6·50) and a new wheel (€12·75) and repaired the bicycle. He then sold it for €75. How much of a profit did he make?

4.
a. 4 x 6 =
b. 2 x 8 =
c. 9 x 5 =
d. 7 x 2 =
e. 9 x 9 =
f. 7 x 8 =
g. 8 x 5 =
h. 7 x 3 =
i. 5 x 5 =
j. 9 x 8 =

5.
a. 7 x 6 =
b. 8 x 6 =
c. 12 x 4 =
d. 6 x 6 =
e. 5 x 1 =
f. 9 x 7 =
g. 7 x 0 =
h. 5 x 6 =
i. 11 x 8 =
j. 4 x 12 =

6.
a. 72 ÷ 8 =
b. 63 ÷ 9 =
c. 36 ÷ 4 =
d. 22 ÷ 2 =
e. 40 ÷ 8 =
f. 42 ÷ 7 =
g. 48 ÷ 6 =
h. 45 ÷ 5 =
i. 54 ÷ 9 =
j. 21 ÷ 3 =

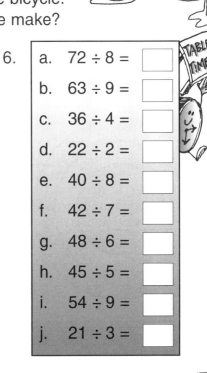

7. **How much will Billy pay if he buys:**
   a. 3 pens @ 11c each and a ruler for 15c?
   b. 4 bars of chocolate @ 12c each and a drink for 32c?
   c. 5 apples @ 9c each and an orange for 15c?
   d. 6 chews @ 8c each and a bag of crisps for 23c?

8. **Find the cost of 2 items if:**
   a. 6 cost 30c
   b. 5 cost 35c
   c. 8 cost 32c
   d. 3 cost 24c
   e. 7 cost 49c
   f. 9 cost 72c
   g. 9 cost 36c
   h. 4 cost 32c
   i. 6 cost 54c

9. **Write a suitable question for each answer.**
   a. 6 oranges
   b. 2 hrs 25 mins
   c. 6 r 1
   d. €232
   e. 9 bars of chocolate

P 1. **Multiplication circles**

Multiply the numbers in sections beside one another and put the product in the next section outside. The first one is done for you.

a.

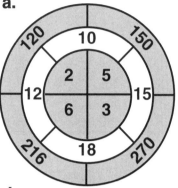

b.

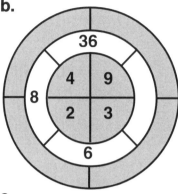

c.

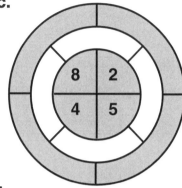

d.

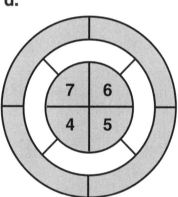

e.

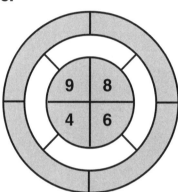

f.

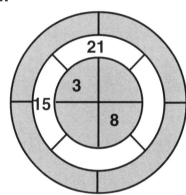

2. a. (23 x 35) ÷ 5 = ☐   b. (45 x 67) ÷ 9 = ☐

3. a. (48 x 95) ÷ 8 = ☐   b. (71 x 26) ÷ 2 = ☐

4. a. (73 x 64) ÷ 8 = ☐   b. (72 x 26) ÷ 9 = ☐

5. How many pages are in 25 volumes of an encyclopaedia if each volume has 376 pages?

PUZZLE POWER

Work these out:

Clue: 7 C in the R
Answer: 7 Colours in the Rainbow

a. 12 N on a C F   b. 6 N on a D
c. 8 S on an O   d. 6 S on a H
e. 5 S on a P   f. 4 S on a R
g. 26 L in the A   h. 12 C in L
i. 52 C in a D   j. 31 D in O
k. 100 Y in a C   l. 3 B M (S H T R)

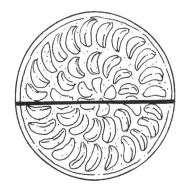

1. **Three apple tarts are on a table.**
   The first is divided into halves.
   The second is divided into quarters.
   The third is divided into eighths.
   a. Which is biggest: $\frac{1}{2}$, $\frac{1}{4}$ or $\frac{1}{8}$?
   b. How many quarters are in one whole?
      How many eighths are in one whole?
   c. How many quarters are in one half?
      How many eighths are in one half?

2. **Say what fraction of each shape below is coloured.**

   a.

   b.

   c.

   d.   e.   f.

[P] 3. Use two rectangles the same size. Divide the first into quarters
   and divide the second into eighths. Shade in $\frac{3}{4}$ of the first and
   shade in $\frac{6}{8}$ of the second. What do you notice?

[P] 4. In how many different ways can you
   divide this square into 8 equal parts?

Can you see that: $\frac{1}{2} = \frac{2}{4} = \frac{4}{8}$ and $\frac{1}{4} = \frac{2}{8}$ and $\frac{3}{4} = \frac{6}{8}$?

1							
$\frac{1}{2}$				$\frac{1}{2}$			
$\frac{1}{4}$		$\frac{1}{4}$		$\frac{1}{4}$		$\frac{1}{4}$	
$\frac{1}{8}$	$\frac{1}{8}$	$\frac{1}{8}$	$\frac{1}{8}$	$\frac{1}{8}$	$\frac{1}{8}$	$\frac{1}{8}$	$\frac{1}{8}$

We say that fractions with the same value are equivalent.

1. **Join 8 Multilink Cubes together to form one unit.**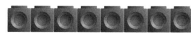

   a. What fraction of the unit is one cube?

   b. What fraction of the unit are:
      i.   2 cubes?   ii.   3 cubes?   iii.   6 cubes?

2. Would you prefer $\frac{3}{4}$ of a chocolate bar or $\frac{7}{8}$ of one?

> **Remember!**
> The symbol < is **less than** and > is **greater than**.

3. **Put the correct symbol (<, > or =) between each pair of fractions:**

   a. $\frac{1}{4} \square \frac{1}{2}$ b. $\frac{1}{8} \square \frac{1}{4}$ c. $\frac{1}{2} \square \frac{1}{8}$ d. $\frac{2}{4} \square \frac{1}{2}$

   e. $\frac{3}{4} \square \frac{1}{2}$ f. $\frac{3}{4} \square \frac{6}{8}$ g. $\frac{3}{8} \square \frac{1}{4}$ h. $\frac{7}{8} \square 1$

   i. $\frac{1}{2} \square \frac{4}{8}$ j. $\frac{3}{8} \square \frac{3}{4}$ k. $\frac{3}{8} \square \frac{1}{2}$ l. $\frac{1}{2} \square \frac{5}{8}$

4. **Put each set of fractions in the correct order. Start with the smallest.**

   a. $\frac{1}{2}$ $\frac{1}{8}$ $\frac{1}{4}$ b. 1 $\frac{1}{2}$ $\frac{1}{8}$ c. $\frac{5}{8}$ $\frac{3}{8}$ $\frac{1}{8}$ d. $\frac{3}{8}$ $\frac{3}{4}$ $\frac{1}{2}$

   e. $\frac{3}{4}$ $\frac{1}{2}$ 1 f. $\frac{1}{2}$ $\frac{3}{4}$ $\frac{7}{8}$ g. $\frac{7}{8}$ $\frac{5}{8}$ $\frac{3}{4}$ h. $\frac{6}{8}$ $\frac{4}{8}$ $\frac{1}{4}$

5. **When can you call 'snap'?**
   a.   **b.**   **c.**   **d.**

   $\frac{1}{2}$ $\frac{2}{4}$ $\frac{5}{8}$ $\frac{3}{4}$ $\frac{1}{8}$ $\frac{2}{4}$ $\frac{4}{8}$ $\frac{1}{2}$

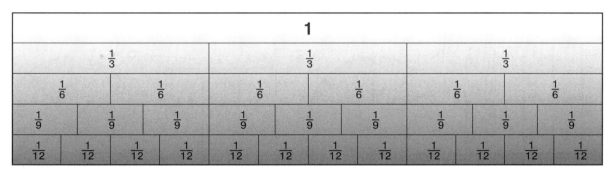

1											
$\frac{1}{3}$				$\frac{1}{3}$				$\frac{1}{3}$			
$\frac{1}{6}$		$\frac{1}{6}$		$\frac{1}{6}$		$\frac{1}{6}$		$\frac{1}{6}$		$\frac{1}{6}$	
$\frac{1}{9}$		$\frac{1}{9}$	$\frac{1}{9}$		$\frac{1}{9}$	$\frac{1}{9}$		$\frac{1}{9}$	$\frac{1}{9}$		$\frac{1}{9}$
$\frac{1}{12}$	$\frac{1}{12}$	$\frac{1}{12}$	$\frac{1}{12}$	$\frac{1}{12}$	$\frac{1}{12}$	$\frac{1}{12}$	$\frac{1}{12}$	$\frac{1}{12}$	$\frac{1}{12}$	$\frac{1}{12}$	$\frac{1}{12}$

1. a. Which is biggest: $\frac{1}{3}$, $\frac{1}{6}$, $\frac{1}{9}$ or $\frac{1}{12}$?

   b. How many thirds are in one whole?

   c. How many sixths are in one whole?

   d. How many twelfths are in one sixth?

   e. How many ninths are in one third?

   f. If you were given the choice between $\frac{4}{9}$, $\frac{5}{12}$ and $\frac{1}{3}$ of a chocolate cake, which would you choose?

2. **Join 12 Multilink Cubes together to make one unit.**

   What fraction of the unit is:

   a. 1 cube?　　　b. 2 cubes?　　　c. 3 cubes?　　　d. 4 cubes?

P 3. **Use four squares and divide them into:**
   a. thirds　　　b. sixths　　　c. ninths　　　d. twelfths

P 4. **Use four circles and divide them into:**
   a. thirds　　　b. sixths　　　c. ninths　　　d. twelfths

5. **What fraction of each of these shapes is coloured?**

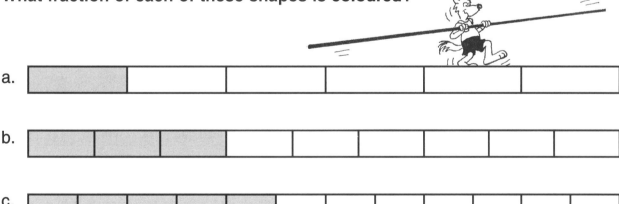

a.

b.

c.

1. **What fraction of each of these shapes is white?**

   a. 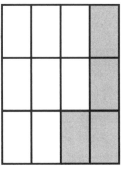 **b.** 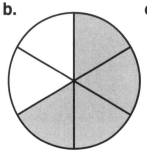 **c.** 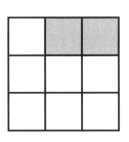 **d.**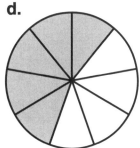

2. **Finish writing these families of equivalent fractions:**

   a. $\frac{1}{3} = \frac{}{6} = \frac{}{9} = \frac{}{12}$ b. $\frac{1}{6} = \frac{}{12}$

   c. $\frac{2}{3} = \frac{}{6} = \frac{}{9} = \frac{}{12}$ d. $\frac{5}{6} = \frac{}{12}$

3. **Put the correct symbol (<, > or =) between each pair of fractions:**

   a. $\frac{1}{6}$ ☐ $\frac{3}{12}$ b. $\frac{5}{6}$ ☐ $\frac{2}{3}$ c. $\frac{2}{3}$ ☐ $\frac{6}{9}$

   d. $\frac{1}{3}$ ☐ $\frac{4}{9}$ e. $\frac{3}{6}$ ☐ $\frac{6}{12}$ f. $\frac{4}{9}$ ☐ $\frac{5}{12}$

   g. 1 ☐ $\frac{11}{12}$ h. $\frac{9}{9}$ ☐ 1 i. $\frac{7}{12}$ ☐ $\frac{4}{6}$

4. **Put these sets of fractions in the correct order. Start with the smallest.**

   a. $\frac{1}{3}$ $\frac{1}{6}$ $\frac{1}{9}$ b. $\frac{1}{12}$ $\frac{1}{3}$ $\frac{1}{6}$ c. $\frac{1}{9}$ $\frac{1}{12}$ $\frac{1}{3}$

   d. $\frac{2}{6}$ $\frac{4}{9}$ $\frac{2}{12}$ e. $\frac{2}{3}$ $\frac{9}{12}$ $\frac{5}{6}$ f. $\frac{9}{9}$ $\frac{2}{3}$ $\frac{11}{12}$

   g. $\frac{5}{12}$ $\frac{1}{12}$ $\frac{4}{12}$ h. $\frac{7}{12}$ 1 $\frac{8}{9}$ i. $\frac{1}{3}$ $\frac{2}{9}$ $\frac{2}{12}$

5. **Answer these questions on tenths.**

1									
$\frac{1}{2}$					$\frac{1}{2}$				
$\frac{1}{5}$		$\frac{1}{5}$		$\frac{1}{5}$		$\frac{1}{5}$		$\frac{1}{5}$	
$\frac{1}{10}$	$\frac{1}{10}$	$\frac{1}{10}$	$\frac{1}{10}$	$\frac{1}{10}$	$\frac{1}{10}$	$\frac{1}{10}$	$\frac{1}{10}$	$\frac{1}{10}$	$\frac{1}{10}$

   a. How many tenths make up 1 whole?

   b. How many fifths make up 1 unit?

   c. How many tenths are equal to $\frac{1}{5}$?

   d. How many tenths are equal to $\frac{1}{2}$?

1. **Join 10 Multilink Cubes together to make one unit.**

   What fraction of the unit is:
   a. 1 cube?   b. 2 cubes?   c. 3 cubes?
   d. 4 cubes?   e. 5 cubes?   f. 6 cubes?

P 2. Use two rectangles. Call one A and the other B.
   Divide rectangle A into fifths. Colour $\frac{2}{5}$ red and $\frac{3}{5}$ blue.
   Divide rectangle B into tenths. Colour $\frac{7}{10}$ blue, $\frac{2}{10}$ red and $\frac{1}{10}$ yellow.

3. **What fraction of each of these shapes is coloured?**

   a.

   b.

   c. 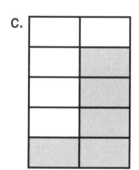   d. 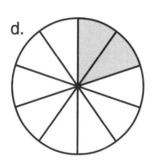   e. 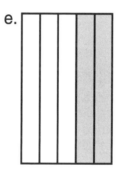   f.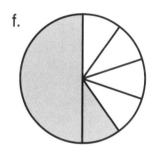

4. **Write the equivalent fractions.**

   a. $\frac{1}{5} = \frac{}{10}$ b. $\frac{2}{5} = \frac{}{10}$ c. $\frac{3}{5} = \frac{}{10}$

   d. $\frac{4}{5} = \frac{}{10}$ e. $\frac{1}{2} = \frac{}{10}$

5. **Put the correct symbol (<, > or =) between these pairs of fractions:**

   a. $\frac{1}{2}$ ☐ $\frac{6}{10}$ b. $\frac{3}{5}$ ☐ $\frac{7}{10}$ c. $\frac{7}{10}$ ☐ $\frac{1}{2}$ d. $\frac{2}{10}$ ☐ $\frac{1}{5}$

   e. $\frac{9}{10}$ ☐ $\frac{4}{5}$ f. $\frac{8}{10}$ ☐ $\frac{4}{5}$ g. 1 ☐ $\frac{9}{10}$ h. $\frac{4}{10}$ ☐ $\frac{1}{2}$

6. **Put these sets of fractions in order. Start with the smallest.**

   a. $\frac{1}{5}$ $\frac{1}{10}$ $\frac{1}{2}$ b. $\frac{9}{10}$ $\frac{3}{10}$ $\frac{7}{10}$ c. $\frac{4}{5}$ $\frac{1}{5}$ 1

   d. 1 $\frac{9}{10}$ $\frac{4}{5}$ e. $\frac{7}{10}$ $\frac{3}{5}$ $\frac{1}{2}$ f. $\frac{5}{5}$ $\frac{8}{10}$ $\frac{1}{2}$

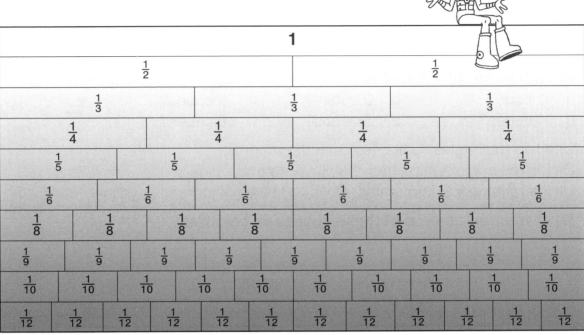

1. **Put these groups of fractions in order. Start with the smallest.**

   a. $\frac{5}{6}$ $\frac{3}{6}$ $\frac{6}{6}$ $\frac{2}{6}$ 　　 b. $\frac{9}{10}$ $\frac{2}{10}$ $\frac{7}{10}$ $\frac{5}{10}$ 　　 c. $\frac{1}{9}$ $\frac{1}{10}$ $\frac{1}{5}$ $\frac{1}{2}$

   d. $\frac{3}{9}$ $\frac{2}{9}$ $\frac{4}{9}$ $\frac{7}{9}$ 　　 e. $\frac{7}{8}$ $\frac{3}{8}$ $\frac{1}{8}$ $\frac{4}{8}$ 　　 f. $\frac{3}{8}$ $\frac{3}{12}$ $\frac{3}{3}$ $\frac{3}{4}$

   g. $\frac{3}{12}$ $\frac{9}{12}$ $\frac{11}{12}$ $\frac{7}{12}$ 　　 h. $\frac{1}{3}$ $\frac{1}{12}$ $\frac{1}{8}$ $\frac{1}{6}$ 　　 i. $\frac{5}{6}$ $\frac{5}{10}$ $\frac{5}{12}$ $\frac{5}{8}$

2. You have five friends coming to see you and you have bought your favourite cake. Into how many equal pieces should you cut the cake if you wish to share it with them?

P 3. **Use your tangram sheet.**

   a. What fraction of the big square does the little square take up?
   b. Make a little square from the two small triangles.
   c. How many big triangles would you need to make the big square?
   d. What fraction of the big square is the big triangle?
   e. What fraction of the small square is a small triangle?
   f. What fraction of the big square is a small triangle?
   g. Form a rectangle (not a square) using all 5 pieces. See if you can do it another way.

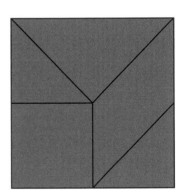

Here we see part of the number line divided into eighths:

0     $\frac{1}{8}$ $\frac{2}{8}$ $\frac{3}{8}$ $\frac{4}{8}$ $\frac{5}{8}$ $\frac{6}{8}$ $\frac{7}{8}$ 1 $1\frac{1}{8}$ $1\frac{2}{8}$ $1\frac{3}{8}$

$\frac{1}{4}$ $\frac{1}{2}$ $\frac{3}{4}$ $1\frac{1}{4}$

Here we see part of the number line divided into sixths:

0     $\frac{1}{6}$ $\frac{2}{6}$ $\frac{3}{6}$ $\frac{4}{6}$ $\frac{5}{6}$ 1 $1\frac{1}{6}$ $1\frac{2}{6}$

$\frac{1}{3}$ $\frac{1}{2}$ $\frac{2}{3}$ $1\frac{1}{3}$

P 1. On a number line, mark the numbers 0 and 1. Divide it into fifths.

P 2. On a number line, mark the numbers 0 and 1. Divide it into tenths.

P 3. On a number line, mark the numbers 0 and 1. Divide it into ninths.

4. Count in quarters from 0 up as far as 6.
   (0 $\frac{1}{4}$ $\frac{1}{2}$ $\frac{3}{4}$ 1 $1\frac{1}{4}$ $1\frac{1}{2}$ ... 6)

5. Count in thirds from 0 to 6.

6. **Write the next three fractions in each of these sequences:**

   a. $\frac{4}{9}$, $\frac{5}{9}$, $\frac{6}{9}$, $\frac{7}{9}$, $\frac{8}{9}$,   ___, ___, ___

   b. $\frac{3}{10}$, $\frac{2}{5}$, $\frac{1}{2}$, $\frac{3}{5}$, $\frac{7}{10}$,   ___, ___, ___

   c. $\frac{1}{8}$, $\frac{1}{4}$, $\frac{3}{8}$, $\frac{1}{2}$, $\frac{5}{8}$,   ___, ___, ___

7. Count in tenths from 3 to 5.

8. **Which is bigger?**

   a. $3\frac{1}{4}$ or 3?   b. $7\frac{1}{2}$ or 8?   c. $6\frac{1}{4}$ or $5\frac{3}{4}$?

PUZZLE POWER

The word **half** is very often used. Can you figure out the missing words?

half-?	30 minutes.
half-?	when football teams change ends.
half-?	6
half-?	when a flag is flown low after someone has died.
half-?	wrestling hold.
half-?	not quite a fullback.

1. a.   What fraction of the above shape is coloured?
   b.   What **decimal fraction** of the shape is coloured?

2. a.   What decimal fraction of each 100 square is coloured?
   b.   How much of each 100 square is not coloured?
        Write your answer as a decimal.

A	B	C

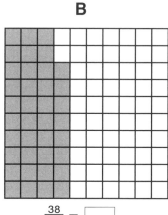
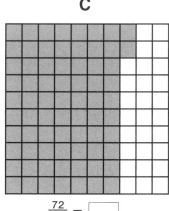

$\frac{64}{100} = 0.64$ $\frac{38}{100} = \boxed{}$ $\frac{72}{100} = \boxed{}$

P 3. **Use three squares like the ones above.**
   Label them A, B and C.

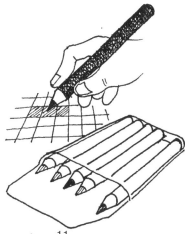

   A   Colour 0·24 red. Colour the rest yellow.
          How much is yellow?
   B   Colour 0·31 red and 0·27 green.
          Colour the rest yellow. How much is yellow?
   C   Colour 0·17 red, 0·37 blue and 0·42 green.
          Colour the rest yellow. How much is yellow?

4. **Write each of these as a decimal:**
   a. $\frac{3}{100}$ b. $\frac{5}{100}$ c. $\frac{7}{100}$ d. $\frac{11}{100}$

   e. $\frac{19}{100}$ f. $\frac{27}{100}$ g. $\frac{99}{100}$ h. $\frac{36}{100}$

5. **Write each of these as a fraction:**
   a. 0·07   b. 0·09   c. 0·12   d. 0·17

   e. 0·38   f. 0·87   g. 0·93   h. 0·75

DECIMALS

We use decimals when we are dealing with money. There are 100 cent in a euro. 1c = one hundredth ($\frac{1}{100}$) of a euro = €0·01

1. a. 99c = € ☐   b. 87c = € ☐   c. 50c = € ☐   d. 7c = € ☐

2. You can see from the picture that $\frac{1}{10}$ = 0·1 = $\frac{10}{100}$ = 0·10.
   In the same way $\frac{2}{10}$ = 0·2 = $\frac{20}{100}$ = 0·20.
   Complete these:

		$\frac{3}{10}$	= 0·3	= $\frac{30}{100}$	= ☐
		$\frac{4}{10}$	= 0·4	= ☐	= ☐
$\frac{1}{2}$	=	$\frac{5}{10}$	= ☐	= ☐	= ☐
		$\frac{6}{10}$	= ☐	= ☐	= ☐
		$\frac{7}{10}$	= ☐	= ☐	= ☐
		$\frac{8}{10}$	= ☐	= ☐	= ☐

Remember! $\frac{1}{2}$ = 0·5 $\frac{1}{4}$ = 0·25 $\frac{3}{4}$ = 0·75

3. **A girl was running a 100-metre race but she fell after running only 63 metres.**
   a. How many metres had she left to run?
   b. Write this as a decimal fraction of the complete distance.

4. There are 100 cent in a euro.
   What decimal fraction of a euro is 41 cent?

5. **Mrs Murphy won €100 in a raffle. She spent €93.**
   a. How much had she left?
   b. Write this as a decimal fraction of all her prize money.

6. **There were 100 cars in a car park. 23 were blue, 17 were yellow, 14 were white, 39 were red and the rest were green.**
   a. How many were green?
   b. Write this as a decimal fraction of all the cars.

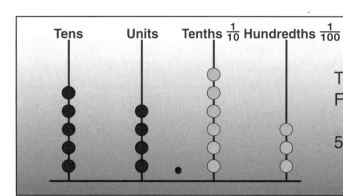

Tens   Units   Tenths $\frac{1}{10}$ Hundredths $\frac{1}{100}$

The number shown here is 54·63.
Fifty-four point six three.

$50 + 4 + \frac{6}{10} + \frac{3}{100}$

1. **Write the number shown by each of these Abacus pictures:**

a. Tens   Units $\frac{1}{10}$ $\frac{1}{100}$

b. Tens   Units $\frac{1}{10}$ $\frac{1}{100}$

c. Tens   Units $\frac{1}{10}$ $\frac{1}{100}$

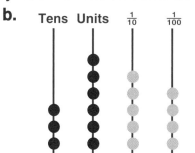

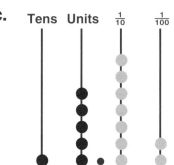

d. Tens   Units $\frac{1}{10}$ $\frac{1}{100}$

e. Tens   Units $\frac{1}{10}$ $\frac{1}{100}$

f. Tens   Units $\frac{1}{10}$ $\frac{1}{100}$

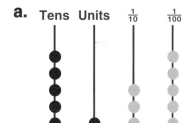

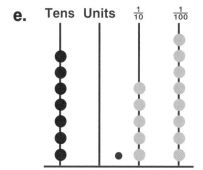

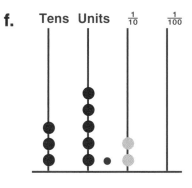

g. Tens   Units $\frac{1}{10}$ $\frac{1}{100}$

h. Tens   Units $\frac{1}{10}$ $\frac{1}{100}$

i. Tens   Units $\frac{1}{10}$ $\frac{1}{100}$

P 2. **Draw abacus pictures to show these numbers:**
   a.   14·06   b.   56·03   c.   4·78   d.   0·67   e.   45·6   f.   32·1

Something is **unnecessary** if you don't need it.
An umbrella is **unnecessary** on a sunny day.
A zero is **unnecessary** if you can leave it out
without changing the value of the number.

1. **Ring the zeros that are unnecessary:**

   a. 90   b. 09   c. 800   d. 708   e. 004   f. 1,002

   g. 8,000   h. 0007   i. 078   j. 1,050   k. 6,008   l. 1,350

2. **Ring the zeros that are unnecessary:**

   a. €5·00   b. €09·78   c. €0800·56   d. €8·05   e. €90·09

3. **Ring the zeros that are unnecessary:**

   a. 1·03   b. 1·30   c. 1·80   d. 1·08   e. 2·0   f. 5·00

   g. 2·09   h. 3·30   i. 0·5   j. 0·08   k. 6·09   l. 4·40

4. Match each number from list **A** with a number of
   the same value from list **B**:

LIST A	6·70	7·6	04·31	6·07	07·06	4·13

LIST B	04·13	7·06	6·7	06·07	7·60	4·31

5. **Put the correct sign (<, > or =) between these pairs of numbers:**

   a.   6·8 ☐ 6·80   b. 03·13 ☐ 3·13   c. 0·60 ☐ 0·66

   d. 0·23 ☐ 0·2   e.   0·5   ☐ 0·05   f.   0·1 ☐ 1·0

   g. 1·23 ☐ 1·32   h.   1·4   ☐ 1·40   i. 1·08 ☐ 1·2

6. **What comes next in each of these patterns?**

   a. 0·2, 0·3, 0·4, 0·5, 0·6, ____   b. 1·13, 1·17, 1·21, 1·25, 1·29, ____

   c. 0·10, 0·12, 0·14, 0·16, 0·18, ____   d. 0·27, 0·30, 0·33, 0·36, 0·39, ____

   e. 0·75, 0·80, 0·85, 0·90, 0·95, ____   f. 0·05, 0·06, 0·07, 0·08, 0·09, ____

Here we see part of the number line.

```
0                                                    10
|   1   2   3   4   5   6   7   8   9   |   11
```

Here we can see the magnified part of the number line between 0 and 1.

```
0                                                     1
|   0·1  0·2  0·3  0·4  0·5  0·6  0·7  0·8  0·9   |
```

If we look more closely at the part between 0 and 0·1 we see:

```
0                                                    0·1
|   0·01 0·02 0·03 0·04 0·05 0·06 0·07 0·08 0·09   |
```

1. What decimal fraction does each letter stand for?

```
1                                                      2
|   1·1  1·2  A   1·4  1·5  B   1·7  1·8  C   |   2·1
```

```
    2                                                3
D   |   2·1  2·2  2·3  E   F   G   2·7  2·8  2·9   |   H
```

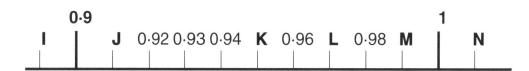

```
    0·9                                              1
I   |   J  0·92 0·93 0·94  K   0·96  L   0·98  M   |   N
```

P 2. Draw the part of the number line that will show the following numbers:
   2·9   3   3·1   3·2   3·3   3·4   3·5   3·6   3·7   3·8   3·9   4   4·1

P 3. Draw the part of the number line that will show the following numbers:
   0·59   0·60   0·61   0·62   0·63   0·64   0·65   0·66
   0·67   0·68   0·69   0·70   0·71

DECIMAL ALLSORTS

1. **Put these sets of numbers in order starting with the smallest.**

a.	0·7	0·4	0·2	0·3	b.	0·8	0·7	0·1	0·6
c.	1·9	1·1	1·3	1·4	d.	6·5	6·2	6·9	6·4
e.	0·67	0·78	0·91	0·23	f.	0·78	0·57	0·31	0·25
g.	0·67	0·6	0·7	0·71	h.	0·09	0·02	0·3	0·16
i.	0·99	0·9	1	0·89	j.	1·87	2·01	1·9	1·93

2. **Write three numbers between:**

   a. 5 and 6 _____

   b. 1·5 and 1·6 _____

   c. 0·36 and 0·4 _____

   d. 1·8 and 1·84 _____

3. Orla has €3·45, Gwen has €3·40 and Laura has €3·09.
   Who has the most? The person who has most has €_____ **more** than the person who has the least.

4. Which is greater: 0·89 of a cake or 0·9 of a cake?

5. **Is the value of the 4 in each of these numbers:**
   4 hundreds, 4 tens, 4 units, $\frac{4}{10}$ or $\frac{4}{100}$?

   a. 46·31   b. 85·94   c. 14·55   d. 133·49   e. 467·02

6. Which would you prefer: $\frac{1}{4}$ of a chocolate bar or 0·3 of it?

7. **True or false?**

   a. 0·45 > 0·54   b. 0·10 > 0·1   c. 0·88 < 0·8   d. 0·7 = 0·70

   e. 0·51 < $\frac{1}{2}$ f. 0·77 < 0·69   g. 1·80 < 1·8   h. 2·35 < 3·15

8. 0·1 of my money is 30c. How much money do I have?

9. I spent 0·3 of my money in one shop and 0·2 of it in another shop. I then had 65c left. How much money did I start with?

10. 0·01 of my money is 9c. How much money do I have?

11. Declan spent 0·5 of his money on comics and $\frac{1}{4}$ of his money on ice cream.
    He then had 36c left.
    a. How much money did he have at first?
    b. How much did he spend on comics?

1. What patterns do you see in this picture? Can you think of other patterns you see every day in the world around you?

2. Draw the shape that should go in the **last space**.

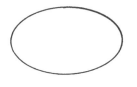

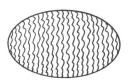

3. **Draw the shape that comes next.**

   a.

   b.
   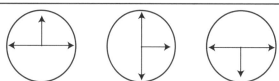

   c.
   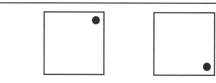

   d.
   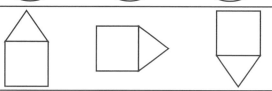
   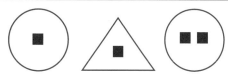

92

1. **Draw the arrow in the coloured square.**

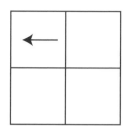 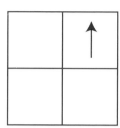 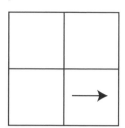 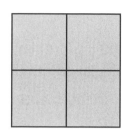

2. **What letter comes next in each of these patterns?**

   a. A B C D E ☐   b. P Q R S T ☐   c. Z Y X W V ☐

   d. B D F H J ☐   e. C F I L O ☐   f. A M B N C ☐

3. **What letter comes next in each row?**

   a. M T W T F S ☐

   b. J F M A M J J ☐

   > **Example:**
   > D R M F S L ☐
   > Answer: T (Doh, Ray, etc.)

4. **What number goes in the blank circle?**

5. **What numbers go in the blank squares?**

6. **Which is the odd one out in each group?**

   a. cow, horse, dog, crow, cat   b. Comet, Moon, Sun, Mars, America

   c. D, 6, R, P, Q   d. Tralee, Rome, London, Paris, Brussels

   e. 7, 6, 48, 80, 54   f. 81, 63, 73, 45, 99

7. **Look at the numbers below and write what comes to mind.**
   Example: 12 – There are 12 in a dozen _or_ there are 12 numbers on a clock face.

   a. 365   b. 52   c. 6   d. 7   e. 10

   f. 20   g. 13   h. 21   i. 11   j. 32

93

1	2	3	4	5	6	7	8	9	10
11	12	13	14	15	16	17	18	19	20
21	22	23	24	25	26	27	28	29	30
31	32	33	34	35	36	37	38	39	40
41	42	43	44	45	46	47	48	49	50
51	52	53	54	55	56	57	58	59	60
61	62	63	64	65	66	67	68	69	70
71	72	73	74	75	76	77	78	79	80
81	82	83	84	85	86	87	88	89	90
91	92	93	94	95	96	97	98	99	100

P 1. On your 100 square, lightly shade all the even numbers.

2. Now count in fours and colour all the multiples of 4 (4, 8, 12, 16...).

3. What do you notice?

P 4. Count in fives. On a different 100 square colour all the multiples (5, 10, 15, 20...) red. Describe the pattern of multiples.

P 5. Count in nines. Colour every 9th square on your 100 square yellow. Write the pattern.

P 6. Count in elevens. Colour every 11th square on your 100 square green. Write the pattern.

7. **On this 100 square some of the boxes are coloured black.**

   a. Write down the numbers that belong in the black boxes.

   b. If the pattern was continued, what other boxes would be coloured black?

1	2	3	4	5	6	■	8	9	10
11	12	13	■	15	16	17	18	19	20
■	22	23	24	25	26	27	■	29	30
31	32	33	34	■	36	37	38	39	40
41	■	43	44	45	46	47	48	49	50
51	52	53	54	55	56	57	58	59	60
61	62	63	64	65	66	67	68	69	70
71	72	73	74	75	76	77	78	79	80
81	82	83	84	85	86	87	88	89	90
91	92	93	94	95	96	97	98	99	100

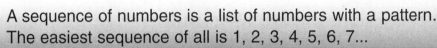

A sequence of numbers is a list of numbers with a pattern. The easiest sequence of all is 1, 2, 3, 4, 5, 6, 7...

Write the next 3 numbers in each sequence.

1. a. 2, 4, 6, 8, 10, 12
   b. 3, 6, 9, 12, 15, 18
   c. 5, 10, 15, 20, 25, 30
   d. 6, 12, 18, 24, 30, 36
   e. 10, 20, 30, 40, 50, 60
   f. 9, 18, 27, 36, 45, 54

2. a. 30, 28, 26, 24, 22, 20
   b. 27, 24, 21, 18, 15, 12
   c. 44, 39, 34, 29, 24, 19
   d. 99, 88, 77, 66, 55, 44
   e. 50, 44, 38, 32, 26, 20
   f. 58, 51, 44, 37, 30, 23

3. a. 103, 107, 111, 115, 119
   b. 68, 74, 80, 86, 92, 98
   c. 57, 64, 71, 78, 85, 92
   d. 241, 244, 247, 250, 253
   e. 342, 351, 360, 369, 378
   f. 550, 558, 566, 574, 582

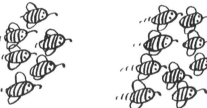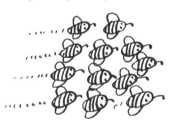

4. a. 986, 988, 990, 992, 994
   b. 982, 985, 988, 991
   c. 2,966, 2,973, 2,980, 2,987
   d. 4,955, 4,964, 4,973, 4,982
   e. 8,034, 8,028, 8,022, 8,016
   f. 6,045, 6,037, 6,029, 6,021

5. a. $\frac{1}{2}, \frac{1}{3}, \frac{1}{4}, \frac{1}{5}, \frac{1}{6}$
   b. 3, 6, 12, 24, 48
   c. 640, 320, 160, 80, 40
   d. 2, 2·2, 2·4, 2·6, 2·8

6. **Can you find the pattern in each row?**

   a. 1,   2,   3,   5,   8,   13
   b. 2,   4,   6,   10,   16,   26
   c. 3,   4,   7,   11,   18,   29
   d. 1,   2,   4,   8,   16
   e. 1,   3,   9,   27,   81
   f. 3,   6,   12,   24,   48

1. Four people played tennis. At the end of the match, each player shook hands with each of the other players. How many handshakes were there altogether?

2. How many handshakes would there be if each tennis player shook hands with each of the other players and with the umpire?

3. This table shows the semi-finalists and finalists in a table-tennis tournament:

SEMI-FINALS	FINAL	WINNERS
Paul & Cathy V Amy & Noel	Paul & Cathy V Nuala & Kevin	Paul & Cathy
Nuala & Kevin V Tony & Claire		

At the end of each match, each player shook hands with the other three players and with the umpire. How many handshakes were there altogether in the semi-finals and final?

4. A number of friends met. When they were saying goodbye they all shook hands with each other. If there were 15 handshakes altogether, how many friends met?

Roman Numerals

Long ago, the Romans had a different system of numbers from the one we use today. Where would you see Roman numerals today?

1 = I	5 = V	9 = IX
2 = II	6 = VI	10 = X
3 = III	7 = VII	20 = XX
4 = IV	8 = VIII	30 = XXX

To write a number in Roman style, bring together the numerals you need.

Examples:

15 = XV   23 = XXIII   29 = IXXX

5. **What numbers are shown by these Roman numerals?**

a. XI   b. XII   c. XIV   d. XVI   e. XVII   f. XXI   g. XXXVI

TARGET TIME

Brenda is playing darts. She throws three darts in each round and all three hit the dartboard. As you can see, it is no ordinary dartboard and after every 3 rounds the board changes. You are given the score that Brenda gets with her three darts. Find where her three darts land. There is sometimes more than one possible answer.

A
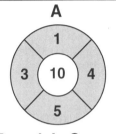

Brenda's Score
Round 1: 6
Round 2: 12
Round 3: 15

B

Brenda's Score
Round 1: 6
Round 2: 19
Round 3: 29

C
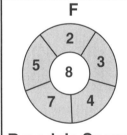

Brenda's Score
Round 1: 7
Round 2: 21
Round 3: 13

D
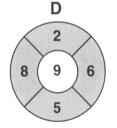

Brenda's Score
Round 1: 18
Round 2: 15
Round 3: 12

E
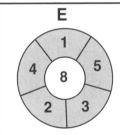

Brenda's Score
Round 1: 20
Round 2: 12
Round 3: 11

F

Brenda's Score
Round 1: 21
Round 2: 17
Round 3: 13

PUZZLE POWER

Here you see 20 lollipop sticks forming 7 squares. Move three of the lollipop sticks in such a way as to make 5 squares instead of 7. You may only move 3 sticks and all 20 sticks must be used. The squares you form will be the same size as the ones you started with.

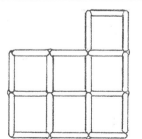

Unit 14 – Length

When measuring a line with your ruler always start at **0**. Some rulers, like the one shown here, have a little space at the beginning. Don't use this space when measuring.

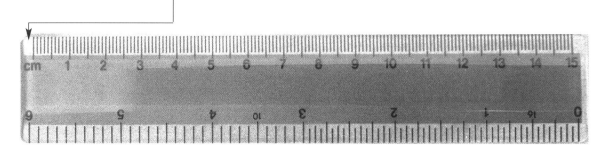

ESTIMATING WITH CENTIMETRES

1. This line is one centimetre in length: ——
   Estimate the length of each of these items in centimetres. Then measure them.

	My Estimate	Actual Length	Difference
Length of maths book	cm	cm	cm
Length of full stick of chalk	cm	cm	cm
Length of my copy	cm	cm	cm
Length of press	cm	cm	cm
Length of my desk	cm	cm	cm
Length of teacher's desk	cm	cm	cm

2. Estimate the length of each of these lines.
   Then measure each line carefully and write the actual length.

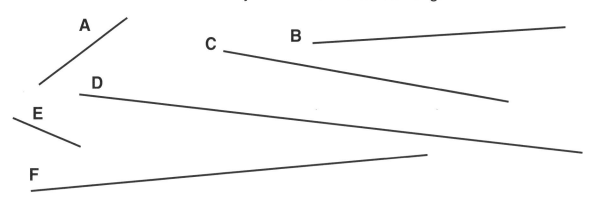

3. **Use your ruler to draw lines of the following lengths:**

   a. 2cm   b. 3cm   c. 5cm   d. 8cm

   e. 10cm   f. 12cm   g. $2\frac{1}{2}$ cm   h. $\frac{1}{2}$ cm

There are **100 centimetres** in a metre.

1. **Estimate** the length of each of these items in **metres**. Then measure them.

	My Estimate	Actual Length	Difference
Length of classroom	m	m	m
Width of classroom	m	m	m
Height of classroom door	m	m	m
Length of windowsill	m	m	m
Length of corridor	m	m	m
Length of playground	m	m	m

2. a. Long ago people sometimes used the length of a person's foot or the span of a hand to measure length. How many times does your hand span the table? Did you get the same answer as your partner?

   b. Would a person with big hands get the same answer as a person with small hands?

   c. Why do we not use our hands and feet for measuring nowadays?

   d. What animal is still measured in hands?

1. **Write centimetres as metres and centimetres.**
   Example: 123cm = **1m 23cm**.

   a. 345cm   b. 645cm   c. 635cm   d. 227cm

   e. 101cm   f. 555cm   g. 363cm   h. 987cm

2. **Write metres and centimetres as centimetres.**
   Example: 2m 34cm = **234cm**.

   a. 2m 45cm   b. 1m 11cm   c. 2m 21cm   d. 4m 45cm

   e. 5m 7cm   f. 2m   g. 4m   h. 11m

3. **Write how many centimetres there are in:**

   a. $3\frac{1}{2}$ m   b. $5\frac{1}{2}$ m   c. $4\frac{1}{4}$ m   d. $9\frac{1}{4}$ m

4. **Write these lengths in metres using a decimal point.**
   Example: 3m 24cm = **3·24m**.

   a. 4m 17cm   b. 3m 56cm   c. 9m 35cm   d. 5m 12cm

   e. 3m 3cm   f. 5m 7cm   g. 3cm   h. 345cm

ADDING AND SUBTRACTING METRES AND CENTIMETRES

Add 8m 34cm to 3m 85cm.	
Change to metres using a decimal point. <div align="center">m 8·34 + 3·85 ──── 12·19m</div>	Add the metres and centimetres separately. <div align="center">8m 34cm + 3m 85cm ──────── 11m 119cm = 12m 19cm</div>

OR

5. a. 3m 56cm + 5m 11cm = ☐   b. 4m 67cm + 4m 23cm = ☐

   c. 8m 51cm + 1m 47cm = ☐   d. 7m 2cm + 3m 8cm = ☐

   e. 5m 22cm + 4m 99cm = ☐   f. 94cm + 1m 7cm = ☐

6. a. 6m 89cm − 4m 55cm = ☐   b. 4m 23cm − 2m 44cm = ☐

   c. 9m 11cm − 7m 34cm = ☐   d. 8m − 5m 43cm = ☐

   e. 6m 3cm − 65cm = ☐   f. 9m − 9cm = ☐

1. a.   7m 45cm – 4m 23cm = [   ]   b.   9m 42cm – 5m 56cm = [   ]

    c.   9m – 4m 56cm = [   ]   d.   6m 45cm – 5m = [   ]

    e.   7m – 7cm = [   ]   f.   9m 9cm – 67cm = [   ]

2. A wall was 8m 60cm long. A builder extended the wall (made it longer) by 4m 50cm. How long is the wall now?

3. Tracy is 1m 35cm tall. Aileen is 7cm taller than Tracy. How tall is Aileen?

4. A bamboo shoot is 3m 90cm tall. If it grows at a rate of 5cm a week, how tall will it be after 4 weeks?

5. In a long-jump competition Sean jumped 2m 4cm and Brian jumped 1m 97cm. How much further did Sean jump?

6. In a high-jump competition, Sarah jumped over the bar which was raised to 98cm. The bar was then raised by 3cm. What height did Sarah have to jump to clear the bar?

7. A blue car is 3m 95cm long. A red car is 3m 77cm long. Would both cars fit into a parking space that measured 7m 50cm?

8. A piece of timber measures 6m 40cm. A piece measuring 1m 23cm and a piece measuring 2m 90cm are cut off. How much timber is left?

THE STORY OF PROCRUSTES

Long ago in Ancient Greece, there lived an innkeeper named Procrustes. He had only one room for guests at his inn and there was only one bed in the room. Procrustes was a strange fellow. He wanted everyone to fit into his bed exactly. He waited until his guest was fast asleep. Then he would sneak into the room. If the guest was too short for the bed he would stretch him, and if he was too long for the bed he would squash him up a bit.

If Procrustes' bed measured exactly 1m 40cm, would anyone in your class be safe in his inn?

4m 35cm x 6		
Change to a decimal and multiply.	OR	Multiply the metres and centimetres separately.

Change to a decimal and multiply.

m
4·3 5
x ₂ ₃ 6
─────
2 6·1 0m

OR

Multiply the metres and centimetres separately.

4m 35cm
x   ₃6
─────────
24m 210cm
= 26m 10cm

1.

a.	b.	c.	d.	e.	f.
m	m	m	m	m	m
3·32	1·23	1·31	2·33	4·24	2·56
x 2	x 5	x 7	x 5	x 9	x 8

2. a. 5·36m ÷ 2 = ☐   b. 5·13m ÷ 3 = ☐   c. 6·15m ÷ 5 = ☐

   d. 4·41m ÷ 9 = ☐   e. 3·08m ÷ 7 = ☐   f. 9·12m ÷ 8 = ☐

3. a. 4m 14cm x 4 = ☐   b. 2m 23cm x 9 = ☐   c. 1m 35cm x 7 = ☐

   d. 4m 16cm x 5 = ☐   e. 17cm x 8 = ☐   f. 4m 44cm x 6 = ☐

4. a. 5m 45cm ÷ 5 = ☐   b. 3m 68cm ÷ 2 = ☐   c. 1m 36cm ÷ 4 = ☐

   d. 5m 31cm ÷ 9 = ☐   e. 6m 23cm ÷ 7 = ☐   f. 4m 32cm ÷ 8 = ☐

5. There are 7 cars parked bumper to bumper in a straight line. If each car is 3m 89cm long what is their total length?

6. A piece of string measuring 6m 48cm is cut into 9 equal pieces. How long is each piece?

7. A guard on duty at a bank walks round the bank 6 times every hour. Every time he walks round he covers $95\frac{1}{2}$ metres. What distance does he travel in an hour?

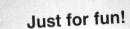

Just for fun!

Q. Why are tall people lazier than short people?

A. Because they're longer in bed!

PERIMETER

The word **perimeter** means **distance around the sides**. A farmer walks around the edge of his wheat field every morning. How far does he walk?
If he starts at a corner and finishes at the same corner he will walk:
60m + 80m + 60m + 80m = 280m.

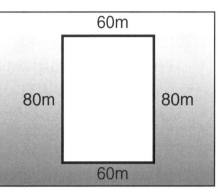

60m
80m   80m
60m

1. **Work out the perimeter of each of these shapes:**

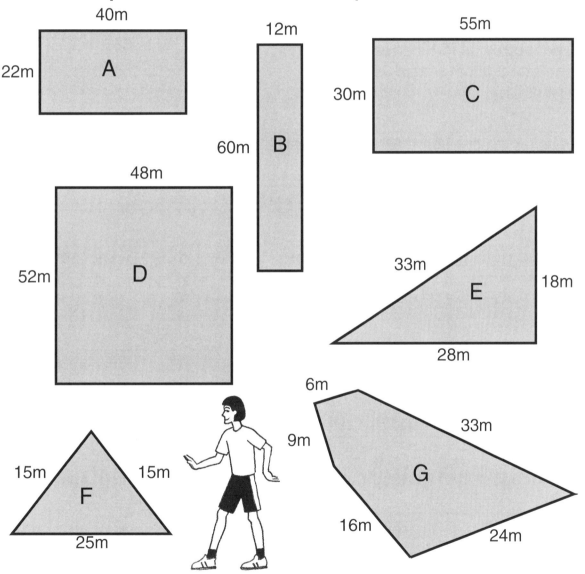

A — 40m, 22m

B — 12m, 60m

C — 55m, 30m

D — 48m, 52m

E — 33m, 18m, 28m

F — 15m, 15m, 25m

G — 6m, 9m, 33m, 16m, 24m

2. A hedge measuring 76m goes all the way around a square garden. What length is each side of the garden?

There are 1,000 metres in a kilometre. If you walked quickly you would walk a kilometre in about 10 minutes. Do you live less than or more than a kilometre from school? The fastest runners in the world can run 1 kilometre in just over 2 minutes! The fastest swimmers in the world can swim 1 kilometre in 10 minutes!

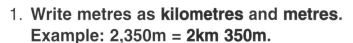

1. **Write metres as kilometres and metres.**
   Example: 2,350m = 2km 350m.

a. 4,550m	b. 5,778m	c. 1,224m
d. 5,660m	e. 1,135m	f. 9,999m

2. **Write kilometres and metres as metres.**
   Example: 2km 331m = 2,331m.

a. 4km 680m	b. 7km 882m	c. 4km 559m
d. 2km 45m	e. 2km 4m	f. 19km 236m

3.

a.	b.	c.	d.	e.
km m	km m	km m	km m	km m
3 445	6 347	2 440	1 449	5 775
+ 4 551	+ 3 556	+ 2 67	+ 4 556	+ 3 8

4.

a.	b.	c.	d.	e.
km m	km m	km m	km m	km m
4 665	2 339	8 446	5 56	7 70
− 3 550	− 2 140	− 6 500	− 3 777	− 5 888

5. **This signpost is in Athlone town.**

Dublin	126km
Cork	219km
Belfast	227km
Waterford	174km

   a. How much further from Athlone is Belfast than Waterford?

   b. How much further from Athlone is Cork than Dublin?

   c. A courier travels from Dublin to Athlone to collect a package. She then delivers it to Cork. How far has she to travel?

THE GREEDY DOG

Do you remember the story of

The Greedy Dog? He dropped

his bone when he tried to grab

the one **reflected** in the water.

Andy drew a square and placed a mirror where
you see the coloured line.
When he looked in the mirror he could
see the entire square.

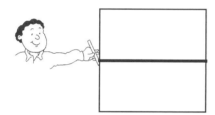

The coloured line is a **line of symmetry**.
It acts like a mirror and restores the
original shape.

1. **Tick the shapes that show a line of symmetry:**

   a. ☐   b. ☐   c. ☐   d. ☐

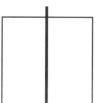   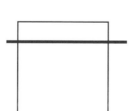   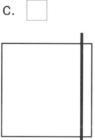   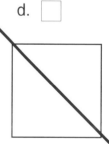

2. How many lines of symmetry has a circle? Draw a circle and find out.

1. Look at the coloured line in each of these shapes.
Tick the shapes that show a line of symmetry.

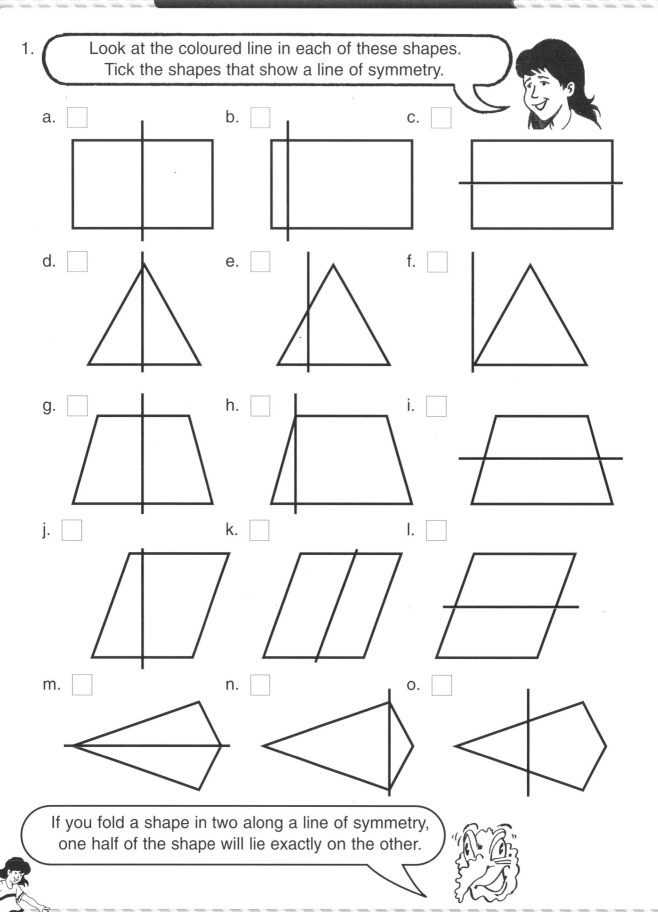

a. ☐   b. ☐   c. ☐

d. ☐   e. ☐   f. ☐

g. ☐   h. ☐   i. ☐

j. ☐   k. ☐   l. ☐

m. ☐   n. ☐   o. ☐

If you fold a shape in two along a line of symmetry,
one half of the shape will lie exactly on the other.

P 1. **Draw a line of symmetry in each of these shapes.**
It may be possible to draw more than one line of symmetry.

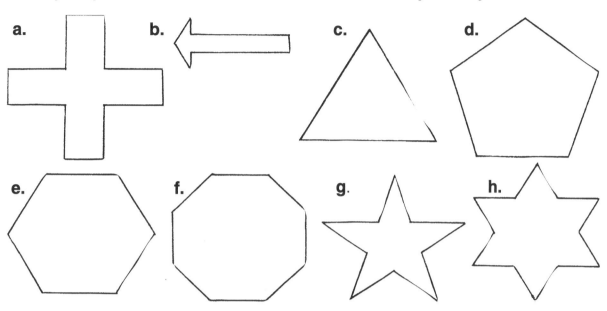

2. **A line of symmetry can be vertical, horizontal or diagonal.**
Is each of these lines of symmetry horizontal, vertical or diagonal?

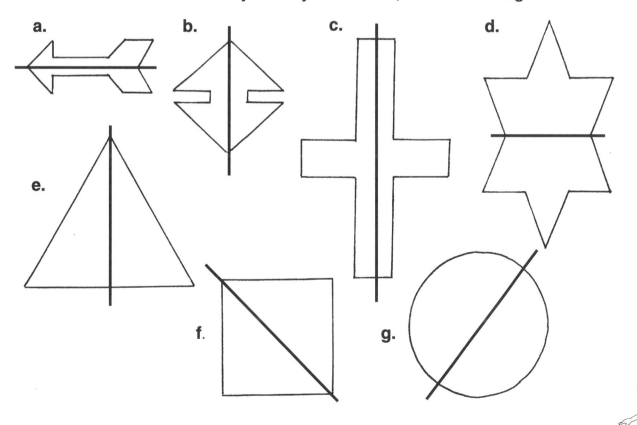

1. Draw the line(s) of symmetry on these letters.
   (Not every letter has a line of symmetry.)

A C E G H I K
L M N P R S T
U V W X Y Z

2. Name 5 objects in the world around you that have symmetry.
   Name 5 objects in the world around you that have no symmetry.

3. **Which of these have symmetry?**
   a. the human body
   b. a butterfly
   c. this gate
   d. a map of Ireland
   e. the Irish flag
   f. a leaf
   g. this door
   h. your hand
   i. the steering wheel in a car
   j. a house

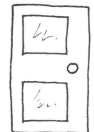

4. Billy got a rectangular piece of paper.
   He folded it in two along a line of symmetry like this:
   Then he opened it up again. He painted one side
   of the paper. He folded the paper over, left it for a few
   moments and then opened it again.
   Was his painting symmetrical?

Detective Time:
The stolen diamonds are hidden somewhere in the kitchen.
Use your symmetry skills to find out where!
Can you code a message like this for your friend?

1. Tick the shields that have symmetry:

a.

b.

c.

d.

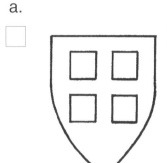

e.

f.

g.

h.

i.

j.

k.

l.

m.

n.

o.

p.

2. Draw 5 coats of arms that show symmetry.

1. Ring the numerals that have symmetry.
   Say if the line of symmetry is vertical or horizontal.
   (It is possible that a numeral could have more than one line of symmetry.)

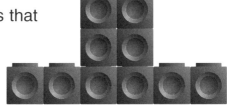

1   2   3   4   5   6   7   8   9   0

2. Use **Multilink Cubes** to make designs that
   show symmetry.

3. **Using the coloured line as a line of symmetry, draw in the missing
   half of each shape.**

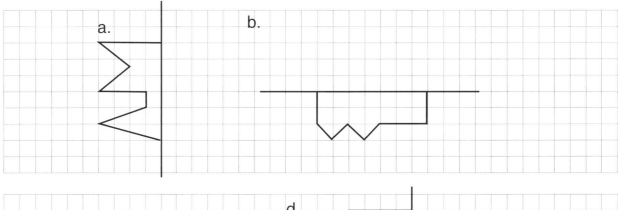

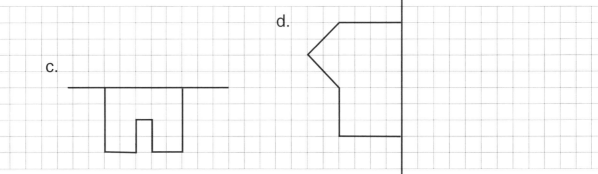

a.

b.

c.

d.

You are in a room with only a candle, a bundle of
wood in the fireplace and a newspaper. It is cold and
dark and you only have one match. What will you
light first?

P **1. Use the coloured line as a line of symmetry to restore the complete shape.**

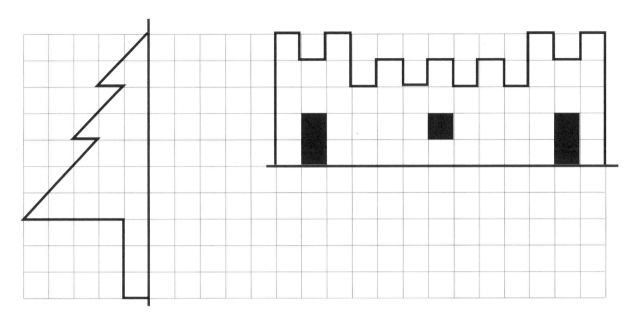

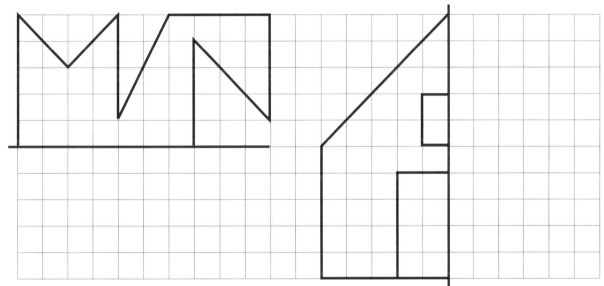

2. Make a symmetrical star. Use A4 paper and draw the lines in pencil. Use only two colours.

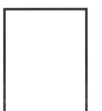 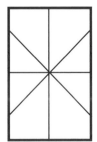 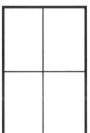 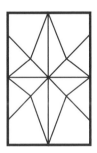 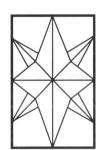 

Let's Look Back (4)

1. **Which is the smallest in each set?**

   a. $\frac{1}{8}$, $\frac{3}{8}$ or $\frac{7}{8}$ b. $\frac{7}{12}$, $\frac{2}{12}$ or $\frac{11}{12}$ c. $\frac{8}{9}$, $\frac{4}{9}$ or $\frac{6}{9}$

   d. $\frac{5}{6}$, $\frac{2}{3}$ or $\frac{9}{12}$ e. $\frac{3}{8}$, $\frac{1}{4}$ or $\frac{1}{2}$ f. $\frac{1}{5}$, $\frac{3}{10}$ or $\frac{1}{2}$

2. **Which is the greatest in each set?**

   a. 0·6, 0·3 or 0·9   b. 0·09, 0·07 or 0·08   c. 0·45, 0·89 or 0·11

   d. 0·12, 0·31 or 0·21   e. 0·5, 0·55 or 0·05   f. 0·13, 0·3 or 0·31

3. How many centimetres are there in one metre?

4. How many metres are there in one kilometre?

5. Write 9m 36cm as a decimal.

6. Write 8m 7cm as a decimal.

7. Write 6·3m in metres and centimetres.

8. What is the perimeter of this square garden?

9. Name any number between 0·6 and 0·7.

10. Name a fraction greater than $\frac{1}{4}$ and less than $\frac{1}{2}$.

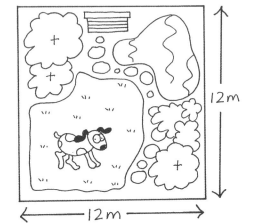

12m

12m

11.
   a. 4 x 7 =
   b. 2 x 9 =
   c. 9 x 6 =
   d. 9 x 3 =
   e. 8 x 9 =
   f. 6 x 8 =
   g. 8 x 4 =
   h. 7 x 7 =
   i. 5 x 9 =
   j. 12 x 9 =

12.
   a. 7 x 3 =
   b. 8 x 8 =
   c. 12 x 5 =
   d. 7 x 6 =
   e. 8 x 1 =
   f. 4 x 12 =
   g. 11 x 0 =
   h. 12 x 6 =
   i. 7 x 8 =
   j. 8 x 12 =

13.
   a. 96 ÷ 8 =
   b. 72 ÷ 9 =
   c. 44 ÷ 4 =
   d. 26 ÷ 2 =
   e. 56 ÷ 8 =
   f. 63 ÷ 7 =
   g. 54 ÷ 6 =
   h. 60 ÷ 5 =
   i. 99 ÷ 9 =
   j. 36 ÷ 3 =

1. Write another fraction that is equivalent to each of these:

$\frac{1}{2}$　$\frac{1}{3}$　$\frac{1}{4}$　$\frac{1}{5}$　$\frac{1}{6}$　$\frac{3}{4}$　$\frac{10}{12}$　$\frac{8}{10}$　$\frac{6}{10}$　$\frac{8}{12}$

2. Write the number that comes next in each of these:
a. 970, 979, 988, 997, ___
b. 0·31, 0·34, 0·37, 0·40, ___
c. 2·23, 2·16, 2·09, 2·02, ___

3. a. 5m 39cm + 2m 56cm = ☐　　b. 2m 78cm + 2m 38cm = ☐

c. 4m 6cm + 5m 56cm = ☐　　d. 7m + 3m 45cm = ☐

4. a. 9m 45cm − 4m 56cm = ☐　　b. 6m 45cm − 5m = ☐

c. 7m − 7cm = ☐　　d. 9m 9cm − 67cm = ☐

5. a. 4m 57cm x 5 = ☐　　b. 2m 17cm x 8 = ☐

c. 2m 5cm x 6 = ☐　　d. 139cm x 9 = ☐

6. a. 5m 65cm ÷ 5 = ☐　　b. 3m 98cm ÷ 2 = ☐

c. 5m 76cm ÷ 9 = ☐　　d. 6m 44cm ÷ 7 = ☐

7. How many lines of symmetry can be drawn in a rectangle?

8. Write any number between 1·3 and 1·4.

9. How much will Billy pay for one if:
a. 4 copies cost 80c?　　b. 7 Fizz Bags cost 56c?
c. 5 pencils cost 60c?　　d. 6 chocolate bars cost 54c?
e. 7 rulers cost 63c?　　f. 9 oranges cost €1·08?

10. 1 metre of ribbon costs 24c. How much will Billy pay for:
a. 2 metres?　　b. $\frac{1}{2}$ metre?
c. 3 metres?　　d. $\frac{1}{4}$ metre?

The line drawn here is exactly 10cm in length:

_____

1. **Estimate whether each line below is less than 10cm, 10cm, or greater than 10cm.**
   Record your findings on a chart.
   Measure each line and check your estimates.

Less than 10cm	10cm	Greater than 10cm	Measurement

a.

b.

c.

d.

e.

f.

2. **Find the pattern in each of these circles and fill in the missing numbers.**

a.  b.   c.  d. 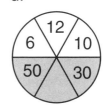 e.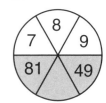

3. Maeve's brother is 11 years older than she is. In 5 years' time, he will be double her age. How old is Maeve?

4. **True or false or may be true?**
   Kenneth is taller than Terry. Terry is not as tall as Paul.
   Paul is taller than Kenneth.

You will need: Multilink Cubes or counters.

1. Count out 24 **Multilink Cubes** and place them in front of you.
   Divide them into 2 equal groups.
   How many are in each group?
   We can see that half of 24 is 12. $\frac{1}{2}$ of 24 = 12.
   Show your answer in your copy book by drawing a picture.

2. Now divide your 24 **Multilink Cubes** into 3 equal groups.
   How many are in each group?
   We can see that one third of 24 is 8. $\frac{1}{3}$ of 24 = 8.
   Show your answer in your copy book by drawing a picture.

3. Divide 24 **Multilink Cubes** into 4 equal groups. $\frac{1}{4}$ of 24 = _____

4. Divide 24 **Multilink Cubes** into 6 equal groups. $\frac{1}{6}$ of 24 = _____

5. Divide 24 **Multilink Cubes** into 8 equal groups. $\frac{1}{8}$ of 24 = _____

6. Divide 15 **Multilink Cubes** into 5 equal groups. $\frac{1}{5}$ of 15 = _____

7. Divide 21 **Multilink Cubes** into 3 equal groups. $\frac{1}{3}$ of 21 = _____

8. Divide 18 **Multilink Cubes** into 6 equal groups. $\frac{1}{6}$ of 18 = _____

P 9. **Colour $\frac{1}{3}$ of each set of shapes.**

a.

b.

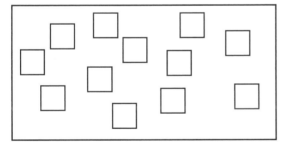
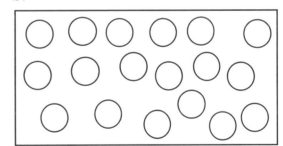

c.

1. a. $\frac{1}{2}$ of 18   b. $\frac{1}{5}$ of 45   c. $\frac{1}{5}$ of 60
    d. $\frac{1}{3}$ of 21   e. $\frac{1}{8}$ of 48   f. $\frac{1}{4}$ of 36

2. a. $\frac{1}{5}$ of 35   b. $\frac{1}{10}$ of 60   c. $\frac{1}{9}$ of 63
    d. $\frac{1}{6}$ of 30   e. $\frac{1}{2}$ of 44   f. $\frac{1}{10}$ of 90

3. a. $\frac{1}{9}$ of 36   b. $\frac{1}{12}$ of 36   c. $\frac{1}{12}$ of 48
    d. $\frac{1}{10}$ of 40   e. $\frac{1}{3}$ of 33   f. $\frac{1}{8}$ of 64

4. a. $\frac{1}{4}$ of 32   b. $\frac{1}{10}$ of 70   c. $\frac{1}{5}$ of 55
    d. $\frac{1}{6}$ of 42   e. $\frac{1}{8}$ of 72   f. $\frac{1}{4}$ of 100

5. John has 24 sweets. If he eats half of them, how many has he left?

6. A nurse has 24 days' holiday in a year. If he took $\frac{1}{3}$ of them in March, how many days did he take? How many days has he left?

7. There are 72 cars in a car park. If $\frac{1}{8}$ of them are green, how many cars are green? How many are not green?

8. If it rained on $\frac{1}{3}$ of the days in April, on how many days did it not rain?

9. There are 441 pages in a book. Conor has read $\frac{1}{3}$ of the book. How many pages has he read? How many pages has he left to read?

10.
A video runs for 1 hour 12 minutes. Clare was $\frac{1}{4}$ of her way through the video when the phone rang and she had to stop the video. For how many more minutes has the video to run?

11. One evening, 372 people attended a concert. Of these people, $\frac{1}{3}$ were men, $\frac{1}{4}$ were women and the rest were children. How many children were there?

12. A milk van delivers milk to 345 houses. One morning $\frac{1}{5}$ of the round was completed when it got a puncture. How many deliveries had the van still to make?

13. Farmer Brown has 234 animals on his farm. If $\frac{1}{9}$ of these animals are sheep, how many are not sheep?

1. Select 24 **Multilink Cubes** and divide them into 4 groups of 6.
   Put 3 of these groups to one side.
   How many **Multilink Cubes** did you put to one side?
   Each group is $\frac{1}{4}$ of your **Multilink Cubes**. You have 3 groups.
   So $\frac{3}{4}$ of 24 = 18.

2. Use your **Multilink Cubes** to help you to finish each of these:

   a. $\frac{1}{3}$ of 24 is $\boxed{8}$ b. $\frac{2}{3}$ of 24 = $\boxed{}$

   c. $\frac{1}{6}$ of 24 is $\boxed{}$ d. $\frac{5}{6}$ of 24 = $\boxed{}$

   e. $\frac{1}{5}$ of 30 is $\boxed{}$ f. $\frac{3}{5}$ of 30 = $\boxed{}$

   g. $\frac{1}{4}$ of 28 is $\boxed{}$ h. $\frac{3}{4}$ of 28 = $\boxed{}$

   i. $\frac{1}{9}$ of 27 is $\boxed{}$ j. $\frac{3}{9}$ of 27 = $\boxed{}$

   k. $\frac{1}{10}$ of 20 is $\boxed{}$ l. $\frac{7}{10}$ of 20 = $\boxed{}$

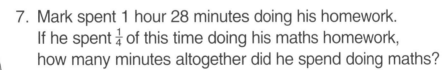

3. a. $\frac{2}{3}$ of 18   b. $\frac{4}{5}$ of 45   c. $\frac{2}{5}$ of 60

   d. $\frac{2}{3}$ of 21   e. $\frac{7}{8}$ of 48   f. $\frac{3}{4}$ of 36

4. a. $\frac{4}{5}$ of 35   b. $\frac{7}{10}$ of 60   c. $\frac{2}{9}$ of 63

   d. $\frac{5}{6}$ of 30   e. $\frac{3}{8}$ of 32   f. $\frac{9}{10}$ of 90

5. a. $\frac{4}{9}$ of 36   b. $\frac{11}{12}$ of 36   c. $\frac{11}{12}$ of 48

   d. $\frac{7}{10}$ of 40   e. $\frac{2}{3}$ of 33   f. $\frac{7}{8}$ of 64

6. a. $\frac{3}{4}$ of 32   b. $\frac{9}{10}$ of 70   c. $\frac{2}{3}$ of 36

   d. $\frac{5}{6}$ of 42   e. $\frac{7}{8}$ of 72   f. $\frac{3}{4}$ of 100

7. Mark spent 1 hour 28 minutes doing his homework.
   If he spent $\frac{1}{4}$ of this time doing his maths homework,
   how many minutes altogether did he spend doing maths?

8. A gardener grew 72 rose bushes one year.
   Of these, $\frac{2}{9}$ died. How many rose bushes died?
   How many did not die?

9. Aileen collects cards. She had 48 in her collection.
   She lost $\frac{3}{8}$ of them. How many has she left?

10. There were 45 trees in a forest. After a bad storm, only $\frac{2}{5}$ of
    them were left standing. How many were blown down?

1. A library has 965 books. Of these, $\frac{2}{5}$ are out on loan. How many are out on loan?

2. A newsagent sold 873 newspapers one day. If $\frac{7}{9}$ of these were morning papers and the rest were evening papers, how many evening papers did she sell?

3. There are 477 children in a school. If $\frac{5}{9}$ of them are boys, how many are girls?

4.  A baker had 576kg of flour. He used $\frac{3}{8}$ of it making cakes and $\frac{1}{2}$ of it making bread. How much flour has he left?

5. A mechanic ordered 744 new car parts. Of these new parts, $\frac{3}{8}$ were faulty. How many were in perfect condition?

Sarah had a necklace with lots of beads. One day the necklace snapped and most of the beads fell off. There were 9 left on the cord. This was only $\frac{1}{3}$ of the full number. How many beads should there be altogether?

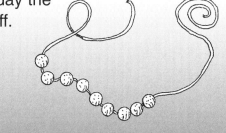

$\frac{1}{3}$ = 9

So $\frac{3}{3}$ = 27

---

6. **Find the whole amount if:**
   a. $\frac{1}{2}$ of it is 9
   b. $\frac{1}{3}$ of it is 8
   c. $\frac{1}{4}$ of it is 10
   d. $\frac{1}{5}$ of it is 11
   e. $\frac{1}{8}$ of it is 5
   f. $\frac{1}{10}$ of it is 7
   g. $\frac{1}{12}$ of it is 6
   h. $\frac{1}{6}$ of it is 8
   i. $\frac{1}{4}$ of it is 8
   j. $\frac{1}{3}$ of it is 11
   k. $\frac{1}{8}$ of it is 7
   l. $\frac{1}{12}$ of it is 4

7. Catherine spent $\frac{1}{3}$ of her homework time learning history. If she spent 25 minutes learning history, how long did she spend at her homework?

8. A cake is cut into 5 equal slices. If each slice weighs 120 grammes what is the weight of the full cake?

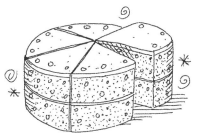

Anna is reading the newspaper. She has read 8 pages of it. This is $\frac{2}{3}$ of the newspaper. How many pages are in the newspaper altogether? This is $\frac{2}{3}$ of the newspaper.	$\frac{2}{3} = 8$
So $\frac{1}{3}$ of the newspaper is	$\frac{1}{3} = 4$
Altogether there are 12 pages in the newspaper.	$\frac{3}{3} = 12$

1. **Find the whole amount if:**

   a. $\frac{2}{3}$ of it is 10

   b. $\frac{3}{4}$ of it is 9

   c. $\frac{2}{5}$ of it is 10

   d. $\frac{3}{5}$ of it is 12

   e. $\frac{7}{8}$ of it is 14

   f. $\frac{3}{10}$ of it is 12

   g. $\frac{5}{12}$ of it is 10

   h. $\frac{5}{6}$ of it is 25

   i. $\frac{3}{4}$ of it is 21

   j. $\frac{2}{3}$ of it is 24

   k. $\frac{5}{8}$ of it is 35

   l. $\frac{11}{12}$ of it is 33

2.  Emma spent $\frac{3}{4}$ of her money on an ice cream which cost 48c. How much money did she have before she bought the ice cream?

3. In a basketball game the Giants scored 90 points. They scored $\frac{3}{5}$ of the total number of points scored during the game. How many points were scored altogether in the game?

4. **A swimmer trained twice last Friday: once in the morning and once in the afternoon. She swam $\frac{5}{8}$ of her total number of lengths in the morning. She swam 24 lengths in the afternoon.**

   a. How many lengths did she swim altogether that day?

   b. How many lengths did she swim in the morning?

5. Ian got $\frac{3}{4}$ of his sums right. If he got 7 sums wrong, how many sums did he do?

SPELLING TEST

A teacher gave his class a spelling test last Friday. There were 12 spellings in the test. Mark got 3 wrong and Jim got 4 wrong. What fraction of the spellings did they each get wrong?

3 is $\frac{1}{4}$ of 12   Mark got $\frac{1}{4}$ of his spellings wrong.

4 is $\frac{1}{3}$ of 12   Jim got $\frac{1}{3}$ of his spellings wrong.

1. If you were given 16 sums for homework and you got 8 of them right, what fraction of them would you have got right?

2. A newsagent had 40 newspapers. At the end of the day he had 8 left. What fraction of his newspapers did he not sell?

3. Joanne spent an hour doing her homework last night. If she spent 6 minutes at maths and 12 minutes reading, what fraction of her time did she spend at each of these?

4. a.   5 is ☐ of 10   b.   7 is ☐ of 21   c.   8 is ☐ of 40

    d.   11 is ☐ of 88   e.   9 is ☐ of 36   f.   5 is ☐ of 45

    g.   7 is ☐ of 56   h.   4 is ☐ of 24   i.   13 is ☐ of 26

    j.   12 is ☐ of 48   k.   9 is ☐ of 45   l.   8 is ☐ of 72

PUZZLE POWER

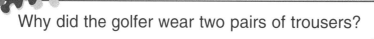

Why did the golfer wear two pairs of trousers?

Match the questions with their correct answers.
Write in the correct letter above the answer.

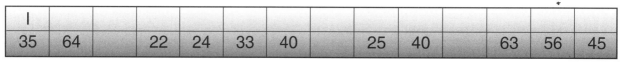

I $\frac{5}{9}$ of 63 = 35   S $\frac{3}{5}$ of 55   N $\frac{8}{9}$ of 72

E $\frac{5}{8}$ of 64   G $\frac{7}{10}$ of 90   O $\frac{7}{8}$ of 64

L $\frac{3}{4}$ of 48   H $\frac{5}{12}$ of 60   C $\frac{11}{12}$ of 24

T $\frac{5}{6}$ of 54   A $\frac{2}{3}$ of 36

I											
35	64		22	24	33	40		25	40		63	56	45

						I					
24		25	56	36	40		35	64		56	64	40

1. **Write each of these fractions as a decimal:**
   a. $\frac{7}{100}$ b. $\frac{9}{100}$ c. $\frac{7}{10}$ d. $\frac{31}{100}$ e. $\frac{9}{10}$ f. $\frac{1}{2}$ g. $\frac{3}{4}$

2. **Write each of these decimals as a fraction:**
   a. 0·09   b. 0·03   c. 0·3   d. 0·67   e. 0·98   f. 0·9   g. 0·25

3. **Complete:**
   a. 71c = € ☐   b. 19c = € ☐   c. 5c = € ☐   d. 99c = € ☐

4. **Write the smallest number in each set.**
   a. 0·8, 0·3 or 0·5   b. 0·13, 0·24 or 0·11   c. 0·45, 0·40 or 0·49
   d. 0·5, 0·51 or 0·15   e. 0·86, 0·89 or 0·8   f. 0·25, 0·08 or 0·36

5. **Hundreds, tens, units, tenths or hundredths?**
   Write the value of the 7 in each of these numbers:
   a. 79·31   b. 85·97   c. 17·55   d. 563·79
   e. 357·02   f. 225·47   g. 725·32   h. 47·68

ADDING DECIMALS

6. a.   3·56   b.   5·67   c.   1·25
    + 4·68   + 6·11   + 10·23
   ‾‾‾‾‾‾   ‾‾‾‾‾‾   ‾‾‾‾‾‾‾

$$
\begin{array}{r}
4\cdot56 \\
+\ 3_1\cdot7_15 \\
\hline
8\cdot31
\end{array}
$$

7. a.   23·55   b.   45·11   c.   78·33
    + 41·26   + 15·59   + 9·03
   ‾‾‾‾‾‾‾   ‾‾‾‾‾‾‾   ‾‾‾‾‾‾‾

8. a.   56·13   b.   48·64   c.   16·00
    + 16·03   + 12·59   + 78·01
   ‾‾‾‾‾‾‾   ‾‾‾‾‾‾‾   ‾‾‾‾‾‾‾

Keep the decimal points underneath one another.

9. a. 113·13   b.   78·23   c.   22·23
    + 226·18   + 20·06   + 88·55
   ‾‾‾‾‾‾‾‾   ‾‾‾‾‾‾‾   ‾‾‾‾‾‾‾

10. a.   45·69   b.   54·59   c.   27·59
     + 15·15   + 26·98   + 45·68
    ‾‾‾‾‾‾‾   ‾‾‾‾‾‾‾   ‾‾‾‾‾‾‾

1. a. 45·23 + 26·11 = ☐   b. 89·12 + 45·36 = ☐

   c. 12·26 + 29·13 = ☐   d. 1·13 + 45·2 = ☐

   e. 4·5 + 87·33 = ☐   f. 45·33 + 7·66 = ☐

2. a. 23 + 0·23 = ☐   b. 5·59 + 15 = ☐

   c. 0·48 + 4·8 = ☐   d. 11·26 + 7·26 + 81·22 = ☐

   e. 7·75 + 15 + 44·55 = ☐   f. 12·45 + 32·32 + 8 = ☐

3. Claire spent €4·56 in one shop and €2·15 in another shop.
   How much did she spend altogether?

4. A horse weighs 352·2kg. A jockey weighs 54·56kg.
   What is the total weight of the horse and the jockey?

5. A petrol tank in a car contained 4·45 litres of petrol.
   The owner went to a garage and added 25 litres of petrol to
   the tank. How many litres does the tank now contain?

6. Sarah saves money every month in the Post Office.
   Look at her Savings Account book and fill in the balance
   in the blank spaces. (The word **deposit** means the amount
   of money she **puts into** her account.)

Date	Deposit	Balance
23 May	€5·00	€5·00
12 June	€3·00	€8·00
31 July	€4·00	€12·00
14 August	€2·50	€14·50
9 September	€2·50	€
17 October	€6·25	€
28 November	€4·75	€
4 December	€1·75	€

1. a. $6·78 - 4·26 =$ ☐ b. $8·45 - 5·12 =$ ☐

   c. $9·55 - 4·47 =$ ☐ d. $10·08 - 6·25 =$ ☐

$$\begin{array}{r} 6·\overset{4}{\cancel{5}}\overset{1}{4} \\ -\ 2·17 \\ \hline 4·37 \end{array}$$

2. a. $36·22 - 23·45 =$ ☐ b. $69·60 - 56·48 =$ ☐

   c. $88·13 - 33·8 =$ ☐ d. $90·5 - 45·01 =$ ☐ e. $99·88 - 45·99 =$ ☐

3. a. $6·23 - 5·11 =$ ☐ b. $9·12 - 5·36 =$ ☐ c. $9·27 - 5·19 =$ ☐

   d. $41·13 - 25·2 =$ ☐ e. $13·92 - 4 =$ ☐ f. $12·01 - 6 =$ ☐

   g. $44 - 0·13 =$ ☐ h. $59 - 1·57 =$ ☐ i. $18·4 - 4·81 =$ ☐

4. What change will I get from €20 if I buy a book that costs €8·95?

5. An elephant and a mahout (elephant driver) together weigh 640·35kg. If the mahout weighs 67kg, how much does the elephant weigh?

6. Alan drank 0·36 litres from a 2 litre bottle of lemonade and James drank 0·25 litres. How much lemonade is left in the bottle?

7. A bag of shopping weighs 8·23kg. A bag of flour weighing 1·75kg and a box of biscuits weighing 2·35kg are taken out of the bag. What is the weight of the bag now?

8. How much will Mrs Power have left from €100 if she buys three items costing €42·50, €35·95 and €9·99?

9. Mr Mooney set out on a 100km journey. He travelled 82·3km by train, 15·06km by car and walked the rest. How far did he walk?

PUZZLE POWER

Katie had an apple pie. Using only 4 straight cuts she was able to cut the pie into 9 pieces. Would you be able to cut it into more than 9 pieces? Remember – only 4 cuts!

Put in your decimal point.

$$\begin{array}{r} 7{\cdot}23 \\ \times \quad {}_1 \ 5 \\ \hline 36{\cdot}15 \end{array}$$

1. a.　4·51　　b.　6·13　　c.　8·14　　d.　9·11　　e.　7·05
　　x　4　　　　x　5　　　　x　8　　　　x　7　　　　x　8

2. a.　2·06　　b.　1·35　　c.　5·05　　d.　3·17　　e.　9·89
　　x　8　　　　x　6　　　　x　7　　　　x　8　　　　x　6

3. **Multiply each of these numbers by 7:**
　a.　3·15　　b.　2·59　　c.　8·01　　d.　7·77

4. How much lemonade is contained in 8 bottles if each bottle holds 1·75 litres?

5. How much will 9 parcels weigh if each parcel weighs 2·45kg?

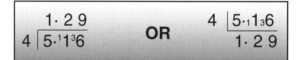

$$\begin{array}{r} 1{\cdot}2\ 9 \\ 4\,\overline{)5{\cdot}{}^11{}^36} \end{array} \qquad \textbf{OR} \qquad \begin{array}{r} 4\,\overline{)5{\cdot}{}^11{}^36} \\ \hline 1{\cdot}2\ 9 \end{array}$$

6. a.　6·25 ÷ 5 = ☐　　b.　8·33 ÷ 7 = ☐　　c.　2·43 ÷ 9 = ☐
　d.　8·22 ÷ 3 = ☐　　e.　6·12 ÷ 6 = ☐　　f.　14·07 ÷ 7 = ☐

7. a.　26·28 ÷ 2 = ☐　　b.　56·25 ÷ 9 = ☐　　c.　33·36 ÷ 4 = ☐
　d.　23·6 ÷ 5 = ☐　　e.　39·1 ÷ 2 = ☐　　f.　41·4 ÷ 4 = ☐

8. The letters in a postperson's bag weigh 4·56kg. If she delivers $\frac{1}{4}$ of her letters, what is the weight of the letters that are still in her bag?

9. Share €19 equally among 4 people so that there is no remainder.

10. Robert had €20. He spent €6·50 on a CD and then he spent half of what he had left on a book. How much has he now?

11. A wheelbarrow and 4 blocks weigh 36·45kg. If the wheelbarrow weighs 15·45kg, how much does one block weigh if all the blocks are the same weight?

Example:

7·2 + 6·4 = ?

Key in:

(7) (·) (2) (+) (6) (·) (4) (=)

The answer 13·6 will appear on your screen.

1. a. 12·56 + 45·11 = ☐
   b. 78·98 − 45·41 = ☐
   c. 24·56 x 8 = ☐
   d. 43·15 ÷ 5 = ☐
   e. 45·26 + 96·63 = ☐
   f. 65·65 − 61·23 = ☐

2. a. 78·15 + 63·25 = ☐
   b. 26·48 − 9·67 = ☐
   c. 45·15 x 3 = ☐
   d. 48·21 ÷ 3 = ☐
   e. 65·06 + 15·57 = ☐
   f. 48·3 − 26·31 = ☐

3. a. 16·5 + 76·09 = ☐
   b. 95·09 − 79·8 = ☐
   c. 76·6 x 9 = ☐
   d. 55·98 ÷ 9 = ☐
   e. 45·59 + 69·9 = ☐
   f. 76·7 − 62·07 = ☐

PUZZLE POWER

To complete the lines of the poem, work out the answer
to each question. Beside each question there is a letter.
In the code grid you will find the answers. Match the questions
with the answers and write in the correct letter above each answer.

The wise old owl lived in

8·64	3·78		8·53	8·64	28·91

The more he saw the less

24·83	81·9		45·37	22·13	8·53	28·91	81·9

The less he spoke the more

					R	
24·83	81·9		24·83	81·9	8·64	28·63	3·48

Let's all be like that wise

						R	
8·53	6·57	3·48		77·12	7·68	28·63	3·48

R   23·5 + 5·13 = 28·63
A   6·78 + 1·86 =
L   3·99 + 2·58 =
D   9·85 − 6·37 =
O   72·01 − 63·48 =

N   100 − 96·22 =
P   87·01 − 64·88 =
K   4·13 x 7 =
E   13·65 x 6 =
B   19·28 x 4 =

I   69·12 ÷ 9 =
H   173·81 ÷ 7 =
S   362·96 ÷ 8 =

1. **Make a chart of things we measure in kilogrammes and grammes.**

We measure these things in kilogrammes and grammes			
1. Sugar	6.	11.	16.
2. Tomatoes	7.	12.	17.
3. Spaghetti	8.	13.	18.
4.	9.	14.	19.
5.	10.	15.	20.

2. **Order these from lightest to heaviest:**
   a. sack of coal, football, tennis ball, school bag (full)
   b. copy, feather, fully grown oak tree, concrete block
   c. lorry, car, jet plane, bicycle
   d. bowling ball, beach ball, bubble, snooker ball
   e. piano, stool, leaf, table
   f. elephant, spider, fox, horse
   g. TV, video recorder, video cassette, CD
   h. ruler, hair, page, metre stick
   i. full stick of chalk, golf ball, balloon, flower petal

3. **Look at each of these weighing scales. Write the weight shown on each:**

a.    b.   c.

Remember!
There are 1,000 grammes in a kilogramme.
Sugar is often sold in 1 kilogramme bags.

Did You Know?
New born babies usually weigh about 3 or 4 kilogrammes.
How much did you weigh when you were born?

You will need a set of kitchen scales.

1. **How many of each of these do you think you would need to make about 1kg in weight?**

   a. apples   b. maths books   c. lunch boxes (full)

   d. oranges   e. maths copies   f. pencil cases

2.  Jimmy asks for one kilogramme of bananas in the supermarket every week. Sometimes he gets 6 bananas, sometimes he gets 7 bananas and sometimes he gets 8 bananas. Why do you think this is so?

3. Collect 5 items such as those listed below. Estimate how many grammes each item weighs. Keep your answers to the nearest 100 grammes. Weigh each item. Compare the actual weight with your estimate and work out the difference between the two. Record your findings on a chart.

	My estimate	Weight	Difference
Maths book	g	g	g
English book	g	g	g
Irish and Geography books	g	g	g
Box of chalk	g	g	g
Lunchbox (full)	g	g	g

4. **Estimate in kilogrammes. Keep your answers to the nearest $\frac{1}{2}$ kg. Choose $\frac{1}{2}$ kg, 1kg, 1$\frac{1}{2}$ kg,...**

	My estimate	Weight	Difference
My school bag	kg	kg	kg
My friend's school bag	kg	kg	kg
Teacher's roll book	kg	kg	kg
4 volumes of encyclopaedia	kg	kg	kg
Football	kg	kg	kg

1. **Write as kilogrammes and grammes. Example: 2,335g = 2kg 335g.**

   a. 6,557g   b. 2,379g   c. 6,198g   d. 9,566g   e. 8,471g

   f. 5,300g   g. 8,451g   h. 4,000g   i. 1,006g   j. 4,090g

2. **Write as grammes. Example: 4kg 456g = 4,456g.**

   a. 5kg 584g   b. 4kg 559g   c. 2kg 113g   d. 1kg 230g   e. 9kg 236g

   f. 4kg 440g   g. 4kg 45g   h. 5kg 7g   i. 2kg 5g   j. 4kg 24g

3.

a.	kg	g		b.	kg	g		c.	kg	g		d.	kg	g
	4	665			2	339			8	446			5	56
	+ 3	550			+ 2	140			+ 6	500			+ 3	777

4.

a.	kg	g		b.	kg	g		c.	kg	g		d.	kg	g
	2	355			4	739			5	256			7	90
	+ 6	780			+ 2	786			+	500			+ 8	70

5. Eileen's school bag weighs 4kg 567g. Her friend Lorraine asked her to carry home her school bag as she was staying back to play in a hockey match. If Lorraine's bag weighs 3kg 482g, what weight did Eileen have to carry home that day?

6. A jockey weighs 55kg 780g. What weight does a racehorse have to carry if he has to carry the jockey and an extra 4kg 440g as a handicap?

7. An angler catches three fish weighing 1kg 340g, 780g and 2kg 560g. What is the total weight of the three fish?

8. An aeroplane allows a passenger to carry a maximum of 15 kilogrammes of luggage. If a passenger has three cases weighing 3kg 600g, 6kg 950g and 4kg 720g, will she be under or over the limit?

Competitive fishing is an activity that involves the use of a weighing scales. The heavier the fish you catch, the better your chance of winning. Horse racing is another sport where scales are used. The jockey has to be weighed before the race. **Can you think of 3 more sports where weight is considered?**

1. a.
kg	g
8	895
− 6	780

b.
kg	g
4	796
− 2	786

c.
kg	g
9	446
− 1	500

d.
kg	g
7	956
− 2	877

e.
kg	g
5	190
− 3	988

2. a.
kg	g
7	359
− 6	585

b.
kg	g
4	000
− 2	386

c.
kg	g
6	256
− 3	762

d.
kg	g
9	41
−	201

e.
kg	g
8	8
− 2	176

3. A bag of cement weighs 10kg. If 3kg 450g of the cement is used, how much cement will be left in the bag?

4. If I spill 345g of sugar from a 2kg bag, how much sugar will be left in the bag?

5. A baker had 10kg of flour. She used $3\frac{3}{4}$ kg of it. How much had she left?

6. Paul and Linda work on a fruit farm. One morning Paul picked 3kg 670g of strawberries and Linda picked 4kg 110g of strawberries. If they want to gather 10kg altogether, how much fruit do they still have to pick?

WEIGHING AN ELEPHANT

Once upon a time in India, three men were having an argument about the weight of an elephant. "It must weigh nearly 100kg," said the first man.

"Nonsense," said the second man.
"It must weigh 500kg."
"You're both wrong," said the third man.
"An elephant weighs almost 1,000kg."
To settle the argument, they decided to find an elephant and weigh it. Finding an elephant was easy, but weighing it was a different matter because, of course, they did not have a weighing scales big enough. They were about to give up when a small boy suggested that they should put the elephant into a small boat that was moored on the river nearby. They did so and the boy made a mark on the boat just at the water level.

The elephant was then taken out. Then they put lots of rocks into the boat until the mark reached the water level once again. All they had to do then was weigh the rocks one by one and add up the weights.

1. **Write these weights as kilogrammes using a decimal point.**
   Example: 6kg 340g = 6·34kg.

   a. 4kg 340g b. 9kg 110g c. 8kg 440g d. 7kg 550g e. 2kg 120g
   f. 1kg 100g g. 5kg 70g h. 2kg 90g i. 1kg 60g j. 9kg 40g
   k. 8kg l. 80g m. 60kg n. 60g o. 30g

2. **Write these weights as kilogrammes and grammes.**
   Example: 4·67kg = 4kg 670g.

   a. 4·34kg b. 7·67kg c. 3·49kg d. 2·13kg e. 2·49kg
   f. 3·59kg g. 2·24kg h. 1·10kg i. 3·3kg j. 5·8kg
   k. 3·6kg l. 2·07kg m. 2,300g n. 6,700g o. 4,590g

4kg 350g x 6		
Change to a decimal and multiply. $\begin{array}{r} \mathbf{kg} \\ 4 \cdot 35 \\ \times \ _2 \ _3 6 \\ \hline 26 \cdot 10 \ \text{kg} \end{array}$	**OR**	Multiply the kg and g separately. $\begin{array}{r} 4\text{kg} \quad 350\text{g} \\ \times \quad _3 \ 6 \\ \hline 24\text{kg} \ 2100\text{g} \\ = 26\text{kg} \quad 100\text{g} \end{array}$

3. a. 3kg 340g x 4 = ☐   b. 3kg 270g x 6 = ☐   c. 5kg 310g x 8 = ☐

4. a. 3kg 120g x 4 = ☐   b. 2kg 330g x 5 = ☐   c. 5kg 450g x 6 = ☐

5. a. 1kg 70g x 9 = ☐   b. 6kg 290g x 7 = ☐   c. 7kg 90g x 8 = ☐

6.
a.	**kg**	b.	**kg**	c.	**kg**	d.	**kg**	e.	**kg**
	5 · 72		1 · 57		3 · 34		2 · 13		2 · 24
	x 2		x 5		x 7		x 5		x 9

7. A bag holds 2kg 500g of potatoes. What will 8 bags of potatoes hold?

8. A box weighs 3kg 560g. What would a dozen boxes weigh?

9. A bag will tear if it holds more than 10kg. If I put 3 items each weighing 1kg 450g, and 2 items each weighing 2kg 800g, into the bag, will the bag tear?

1. a. 5kg 650g ÷ 5 = ☐   b. 3kg 760g ÷ 2 = ☐

2. a. 5kg 940g ÷ 9 = ☐   b. 6kg 90g ÷ 7 = ☐

3. a. 9kg 780g ÷ 6 = ☐   b. 8kg 50g ÷ 7 = ☐

4. If 5 bags of rice weigh 6kg 350g, what is the weight of one bag?

5. How many 9kg bags of potatoes can I fill from 300kg?

6. A family uses 6kg 650g of potatoes in a week. If they eat the same amount of potatoes every day, what weight of potatoes do they eat every day?

7. Roy weighs 30kg on Earth. His weight is different on each of the nine planets of the solar system. To calculate what Roy would weigh on the other planets, multiply his weight by the number beside the planet.

Earth		Roy weighs 30kg on Earth
Mercury	x 0·38	11·4kg (0·38 x 30kg)
Venus	x 0·9	27kg
Mars	x 0·38	
Jupiter	x 2·64	
Saturn	x 1·16	
Uranus	x 0·93	
Neptune	x 1·2	
Pluto	x 0·05	

On which planet does Roy weigh: a. the most? b. the least?
On which two planets does he weigh the same?

PUZZLE POWER

A boat lies on the beach. There is a rope ladder over the side of the boat. The rope ladder has 10 rungs which are 20 centimetres apart. The water is touching the bottom rung. The tide is coming in and is rising at a rate of 40 centimetres an hour. How long will it be before the water reaches the top rung?

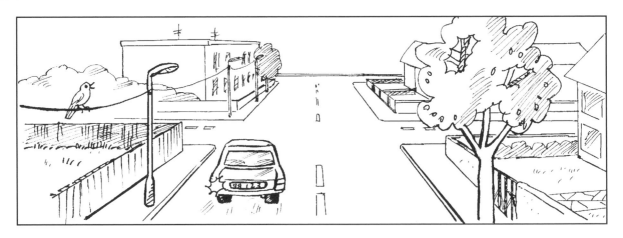

1. **Look at the picture. Choose the most suitable words for the blanks below:**

a.	The car will _____ turn right.	definitely
b.	The car is _____ at a crossroads.	probably
c.	The bird is _____ sitting in the tree.	might
d.	There _____ be a tool kit in the boot of the car.	probably not
e.	The driver of the car is_____ the owner.	definitely not

2. **Look at the picture. Choose the most suitable words for the blank spaces:**

a.	The game is _____ over.	definitely
b.	The ball _____ go into the net.	probably
c.	The score is _____ 50–28.	might
d.	The Giants will _____ win the match.	probably not
e.	The Lofties will _____ win the match.	definitely not

1. Match the sentences.

a.
Tuesday comes immediately before Monday.	Likely
Sunday comes immediately after Saturday.	Unlikely
You will find a 20 euro note on your way home from school today.	Never
It will be cold next January.	Definitely

b.
Christmas Day will fall in December.	Likely
You will eat this evening.	Unlikely
You will fall out of bed tonight.	Never
Easter will fall in July.	Definitely

c.
You will visit London this weekend.	Likely
You will watch TV this weekend.	Unlikely
Some cars are painted blue.	Never
Leaves fall from the trees in spring.	Definitely

d.
You are a boy.	Likely
You will drink something today.	Unlikely
You will eat Christmas pudding this evening.	Never
You are a girl.	Definitely

2. Write sentences that show you understand these words:

a. definitely
b. definitely not
c. probably
d. probably not
e. maybe
f. likely
g. unlikely
h. never

He will definitely fall.

He'll probably fall.

Maybe he'll fall.

133

Many stories are told about people long ago who were able to tell the future. We all know the story of Fionn McCumhaill who put his thumb in his mouth in order to find out anything he wished to know. In Ancient Greece, there was an **oracle** or wise person at Delphi who was able to predict who was going to win a battle.

Unless you are lucky enough to have a magic thumb, or have an **oracle** in your back garden, you cannot predict the future. What you **can** do very often is use your common sense to say what is **likely** to happen in the future.

1. **Look at the cartoons below. Draw what you think will happen next.**

a.

b.

c.

Put the following sentences in order. Start with the one you think is most likely and finish with the one you think is least likely.

1. a. You will see a swallow on your way home from school today.
   b. It will be bright at 1:00 p.m. tomorrow.
   c. You will see a car on your way home from school today.
   d. It will be bright at midnight tonight.

2. a. You will be 21 on your next birthday.
   b. You will see a horse on your way home from school today.
   c. You will see a kangaroo on your way home from school today.
   d. The grass in the fields will still be green tomorrow.

3. a. You will walk home from school this afternoon.
   b. You will drive home from school this afternoon.
   c. You will get the bus home from school this afternoon.
   d. You will get a lift home from school this afternoon.

4. a. You will have cornflakes for dinner today.
   b. You will have potatoes for dinner today.
   c. You will have pasta for dinner today.
   d. A spaceship will land on your roof tonight.

5. **There are 10 Multilink Cubes in a bag. 5 of them are red, 3 are blue and 2 are green. I pick one cube from the bag without looking:**
   a. The cube is blue.
   b. The cube is red.
   c. The cube is yellow.
   d. The cube is green.

6. **Somebody throws a dice:**
   a. The number is a 6.
   b. The number is greater than 1.
   c. The number is greater than 2.
   d. The number is greater than 3.

7. **Teacher thinks of a number between 1 and 100.**
   a. The number is 56.
   b. The number is 458.
   c. The number is less than 100.
   d. The number is less than 20.

1. **Draw a Chance Line like this and mark each event.**

A   B

| | | | | |

Impossible   Unlikely   Maybe   Likely   Definitely

A   A horse will sing.
B   You will sleep tonight.
C   It will be bright tomorrow at two o'clock.
D   You will visit Belfast at the weekend.
E   If you throw a dice the number shown will be 4.
F   If you pick a card from a deck without looking it will be an ace.
G   You will visit the cinema at the weekend.
H   You will see a green car today.
I   The next car you see will be green.
J   It will snow tomorrow.
K   If you toss a coin, the result will be heads.

FIFTY-FIFTY

If you toss a coin there is an equal or 50-50 chance of tossing heads.
There is an equal or 50-50 chance of tossing tails (harps).
If you were to try to predict the colour of the next car to pass the
school, you could choose from lots of colours. There would not be a
50-50 chance of predicting correctly.

2. **Say whether each of these sentences describes a 50-50 chance or not:**
   a.   The next person you see passing the school will be male (man or boy).
   b.   The next car that passes the school will be a Ford.
   c.   Your teacher thinks of any number. The number is odd.
   d.   The next bird you see in the school yard will be a seagull.
   e.   The next baby born in the world will be a girl.
   f.   Your baby sister pressed a key at random
         on your calculator. The key she pressed is ⑦ .
   g.   Your friend has her hands behind her back. She has 50 cent in one
         hand and asks you to guess which hand.
   h.   The next traffic light you see will be red.
   i.   You pick a card from a deck without looking. It is a king.

TOSSING A COIN

P 1. Toss a coin ten times and record the results on a chart like this:

	1st	2nd	3rd	4th	5th	6th	7th	8th	9th	10th
Heads	✔									
Tails		✔	✔							

    a.   How many times did you toss heads?

    b.   How many times did you toss tails?

ROLLING A DICE

P 2. Roll a dice twenty times and record the numbers rolled on a chart like this:

	1st	2nd	3rd	4th	5th	6th	7th	8th	9th	10th
Number rolled	4	3	3	1						
Odd (O) or Even (E)	E	O	O	O						

	11th	12th	13th	14th	15th	16th	17th	18th	19th	20th
Number rolled										
Odd (O) or Even (E)										

    a.   How many rolls were even?

    b.   How many rolls were odd?

SCISSORS, ROCK AND PAPER GAME

P 3. Play this game with a friend. Scissors cuts paper, paper wraps around rock and rock blunts scissors. In your head, choose scissors, rock or paper. Your friend chooses at the same time. On the count of 3, you both make a hand sign to show which you have chosen. Play 10 times and keep a record.

Example:

	1st	2nd	3rd	4th	5th	6th	7th	8th	9th	10th
Kate chose	S	P	P	R	P	R	S	P	P	S
Dan chose	R	R	P	S	S	P	P	P	R	S
Who won?	Dan	Kate	–	Kate	Dan	Dan	Kate	–	Kate	–

    a.   How many times was scissors chosen?

    b.   How many times was rock chosen?

    c.   How many times was paper chosen?

    d.   How many times did you and your friend choose the same thing?

Place 4 **Multilink Cubes** in a bag. One of the cubes should be black, one should be white and two should be red. The bag should not be see-through and should be big enough to allow you to fit your hand inside.

Shake the bag and choose one cube without looking. Record its colour and repeat the action another 19 times. Remember each time to return the cube you take out.

	1st	2nd	3rd	4th	5th	6th	7th	8th	9th	10th
Colour of Cube	B	R	R	W						

	11th	12th	13th	14th	15th	16th	17th	18th	19th	20th
Colour of Cube										

1. a. How many times did you pick a black cube?
   b. How many times did you pick a white cube?
   c. How many times did you pick a red cube?
   d. If you were to pick a cube one more time and were asked to predict its colour, what colour would you choose and why?

2. Look at each spinner. Which colour is: (a) most likely (b) least likely to come up?

A
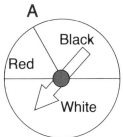

B
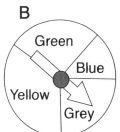

C
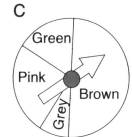

D
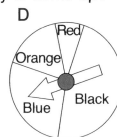

3. **Predict** the answer to each of these questions and then carry out a survey to see if your prediction was right:
   a. Most popular fruit in the class?
   b. Most popular singer or group?
   c. Most popular soccer team?
   d. Most popular TV programme?
   e. Most popular computer game?
   f. Most common lunch item?

ST BRIGID

A story about St Brigid tells how she used her cloak to get land from a local chieftain. St Brigid needed the land in order to build a convent. The crafty chieftain told her that she could have the area of land covered by her cloak! Imagine his surprise when her cloak stretched and stretched until it covered five fields! The chieftain could not go back on his word and had to grant her the **area** covered by her cloak.

1. **Which of these, in your opinion, has the bigger area?**

   a. The cover of your maths book or the cover of your teacher's roll book.

   b. Ireland or Great Britain.

   c. The blackboard or the top surface of your desk.

   d. The classroom floor or your bathroom floor at home.

   e. The local park or the school yard.

   f. County Louth or County Tipperary.

   g. The cover of your maths copy or the cover of a notebook.

   h. The Sahara Desert or County Cork.

   i. The floor of the classroom or the ceiling of the classroom.

   j. A cinema screen or a television screen.

   k. Shape A or Shape B.

   l. Shape C or Shape D.

   m. Shape E or Shape F.

1. Hilda the Handywoman has 8 jobs to do. Unfortunately Hilda knows nothing about area and four of the jobs involve measuring area. Which 4 jobs will Hilda be able to do?

   a. Measure the sitting room and put down a new carpet.

   b. Measure the front garden to sow grass seed.

   c. Put a new skirting board in the kitchen.

   d. Measure and tile the kitchen wall.

   e. Buy enough paint for the kitchen ceiling.

   f. Build a new wall at the end of the back garden.

   g. Put up goal posts for football in the sports field.

   h. Buy ribbon for her Christmas presents.

One square centimetre can also be written as:
1 sq cm or **1cm²**.

2. Draw a **square centimetre** in your copy and colour it.
   Use your set square to make sure that the sides of the square are perpendicular to each other. Each side of the square must be exactly one centimetre.

3. **Find the area of each shape by counting the number of square centimetres.**

   a.

   b.

   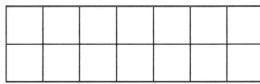

   c.

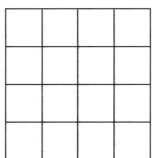

d.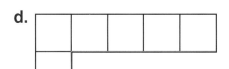
e.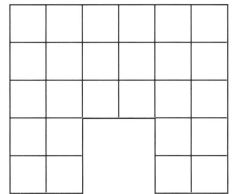
f.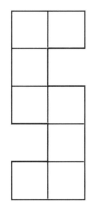

4. On tracing paper, draw a rectangle that is 10cm long and 4cm wide.
   Divide the rectangle into square centimetres, just like the shapes above.
   (You can use this cm² tracing paper in question 5.)
   Into how many square centimetres is the rectangle divided?

5. Look at each of the shapes below. Estimate the area of each shape in
   square centimetres. Then, by covering the shape carefully with your cm²
   tracing paper, find the actual area. Before you start, you could make a
   chart like the one at the bottom of the page.

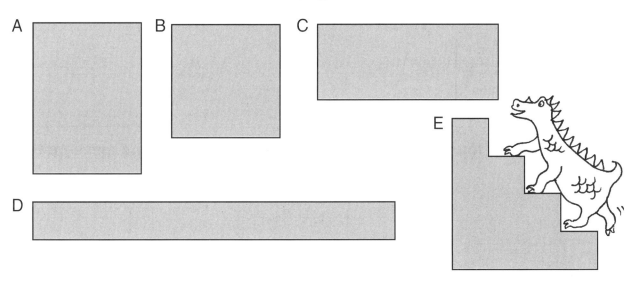

	My estimate	Actual area	Difference
Shape A	cm²	cm²	cm²
Shape B	cm²	cm²	cm²
Shape C	cm²	cm²	cm²
Shape D	cm²	cm²	cm²
Shape E	cm²	cm²	cm²

1. Find the area of these shapes by counting the square centimetres.
   If a line of the shape cuts a square centimetre exactly in half, count
   it as half a cm².

   If more than half of the square centimetre is taken up, count it as 1cm².
   If less than half of the square centimetre is taken up, don't count it at all.

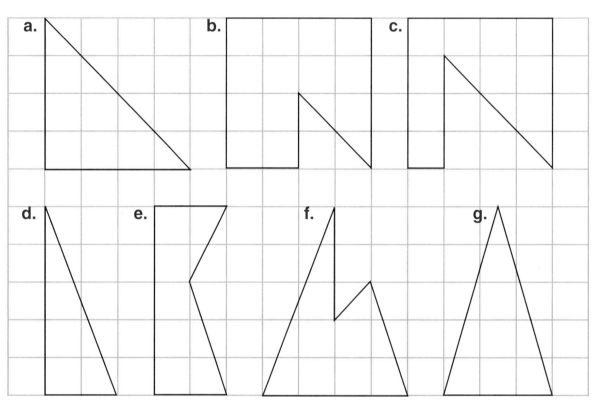

2. **Draw three or four shapes of your own here. Let your friend measure them.**

Tape old newspapers to the floor to mark out a square.
The square must be one metre long and one metre wide.
You may write **1 sq m** or **1m²** but you should always say
square metre.

1. **Is each area less than one square metre or greater than one square metre?**

   a. the classroom

   b. the cover of your maths book

   c. the blackboard

   d. the door into the classroom

   e. the door of the press

   f. a pane of glass in the window

2. **Arrange these groups in order of area starting with the smallest:**

   a. school yard,   classroom,   County Longford,   Leinster.

   b. America,   Ireland,   County Limerick,   Munster.

   c. notice board,   blackboard,   top of your desk,   classroom window.

3. How many maths copies would you need to cover one square metre?

4. How many tiles, each measuring **one square metre,** would you need to cover:
   a. the classroom floor?   b. the school yard?   c. the corridor?

5. Why would we not use square centimetres to measure the area of the classroom?

6. Make a square measuring 1m² of newspaper and cut it
   into two equal pieces. Put them alongside one another
   as you see in the picture.
   Would the area of the rectangle you have just made be
   bigger or smaller than the area of the square?

7. How many square centimetres would you need to
   make a square metre?

8. A woman has a garden with an area of
   240m². In the middle of the garden
   there is a flower bed with an area
   of 42m².
   What is the area of the garden around
   the flower bed?

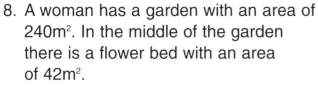

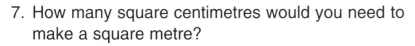

Let's Look Back (5)

1. a. $\frac{1}{2}$ of 12 = ☐   b. $\frac{1}{3}$ of 24 = ☐   c. $\frac{1}{5}$ of 40 = ☐

    d. $\frac{1}{6}$ of 36 = ☐   e. $\frac{1}{9}$ of 45 = ☐   f. $\frac{1}{10}$ of 90 = ☐

    g. $\frac{1}{4}$ of 44 = ☐   h. $\frac{1}{6}$ of 54 = ☐   i. $\frac{1}{5}$ of 55 = ☐

    j. $\frac{1}{8}$ of 56 = ☐   k. $\frac{1}{10}$ of 100 = ☐   l. $\frac{1}{2}$ of 66 = ☐

    m. $\frac{1}{12}$ of 48 = ☐   n. $\frac{1}{3}$ of 39 = ☐   o. $\frac{1}{10}$ of 10 = ☐

    p. $\frac{1}{8}$ of 8 = ☐   q. $\frac{2}{5}$ of 45 = ☐   r. $\frac{3}{4}$ of 24 = ☐

    s. $\frac{4}{9}$ of 18 = ☐   t. $\frac{7}{10}$ of 30 = ☐   u. $\frac{11}{12}$ of 24 = ☐

    v. $\frac{3}{8}$ of 32 = ☐   w. $\frac{2}{3}$ of 33 = ☐   x. $\frac{3}{4}$ of 36 = ☐

2. **Write each fraction as a decimal:**
    a. $\frac{3}{10}$ b. $\frac{7}{10}$ c. $\frac{3}{100}$ d. $\frac{13}{100}$ e. $\frac{99}{100}$ f. $\frac{3}{4}$ g. $\frac{1}{2}$

3. What is $7 - 0\cdot6$?

4. **Which of these is nearest in weight to 1 kilogramme:**
    full bag of coal, stick of chalk, maths copy or 6 bananas?

5. How many grammes are there in 6kg 75g?

6. If you threw a dice, is the number shown more likely to be greater than 4 or less than 4?

7. What units of measurement would I use to measure the perimeter of a garden?

8. What units of measurement would I use to measure the area of a garden?

9. $\frac{1}{6}$ of a number is 12. What is the number?

10. **Tim spent $\frac{4}{5}$ of his money buying a comic which cost 60c.**
    a. How much money did he have before he bought the comic?
    b. How much money has he now?

11. Mark got 20 sums for homework. He got 4 of them wrong. What fraction of his sums did he get wrong?

12. How many toes will you find in a class of 30 pupils?

144

1. a. 6·74   b. 8·49   c. 2·63   d. 9·95   e. 3·08
       + 4·26   + 5·12   + 3·44   + 4·47   + 6·25

2. a. 43·22   b. 88·60   c. 98·03   d. 88·13   e. 90·50
       − 23·45   − 56·48   − 46·17   − 22·80   − 45·04

3. a. 6kg 880g x 4 = ☐   b. 2kg 340g x 6 = ☐

4. a. 4kg 230g ÷ 9 = ☐   b. 7kg 650g ÷ 5 = ☐

5.   A bag of shopping weighed 1kg 467g. Marion added a tin of salmon weighing 138g to the bag and took out an apple weighing 85g. What is the weight of the shopping now?

6. **1kg of carrots costs 24c. How much will Billy pay for:**
    a. 2kg of carrots?   b. 3kg of carrots?   c. $\frac{1}{2}$kg of carrots?
    d. $\frac{1}{4}$kg of carrots?   e. 1$\frac{1}{2}$kg of carrots?   f. 3$\frac{1}{4}$kg of carrots?

7.   **250g of tomatoes costs 32c. How much will Billy pay for:**
    a. 500g of tomatoes?   b. 125g of tomatoes?   c. 1kg of tomatoes?
    d. 1$\frac{1}{4}$kg of tomatoes?   e. 2kg of tomatoes?   f. 1$\frac{1}{2}$kg of tomatoes?

8. **Put in the correct signs: +, −, x, or ÷.**
    a. (5 ☐ 8) ☐ 4 = 17   b. (6 ☐ 7) ☐ 9 = 22
    c. (10 ☐ 2) ☐ 7 = 15   d. (12 ☐ 11) ☐ 2 = 3
    e. (3 ☐ 4) ☐ 5 = 60   f. (30 ☐ 6) ☐ 5 = 1
    g. (4 ☐ 5) ☐ 2 = 10   h. (32 ☐ 8) ☐ 4 = 16
    i. (7 ☐ 6) ☐ 3 = 45   j. (9 ☐ 9) ☐ 81 = 0

9. How many months have 28 days?

PUZZLE POWER

A big polar bear and a little polar bear went fishing one day. The little polar bear was the big polar bear's son but the big polar bear was not the little polar bear's dad. How was this possible?

1. **Match the answers with the correct questions.**
   Write the letters to find the answers to the jokes.

   a.   **How would you tell a dinosaur to hurry up?**

64	28	42	48	T 14	42		84	18	45	28	45	84

T $\frac{2}{5}$ of 35 = $\boxed{14}$ R $\frac{4}{9}$ of 63 = ☐

A $\frac{3}{8}$ of 48 = ☐   O $\frac{7}{12}$ of 72 = ☐

U $\frac{5}{6}$ of 54 = ☐   N $\frac{4}{5}$ of 60 = ☐

S $\frac{7}{8}$ of 96 = ☐   P $\frac{8}{9}$ of 72 = ☐

   b.   **What did one candle say to the other candle?**

			41·85	19·38	418·5	32·06			60·72	345·6

345·6	49·44	418·5		418·5	345·6	21·36	61·88	60·72	49·35	418·5

N   3·56 x 6 = ☐   H   9·87 x 5 = ☐

U   6·18 x 8 = ☐   I   8·84 x 7 = ☐

G   7·59 x 8 = ☐   T   46·5 x 9 = ☐

S   4·58 x 7 = ☐   L   4·65 x 9 = ☐

E   3·23 x 6 = ☐   O   86·4 x 4 = ☐

   c.   **What table is made of paper?**

5·81	31·6	2·36	3·79	5·81	7·13	8·47	98·7	3·79

M   14·16 ÷ 6 = ☐   L   888·3 ÷ 9 = ☐

I   284·4 ÷ 9 = ☐   T   34·86 ÷ 6 = ☐

B   67·76 ÷ 8 = ☐   A   57·04 ÷ 8 = ☐

E   26·53 ÷ 7 = ☐

Unit 21 – Graphs

1. **A group of 25 children were asked, "Which of these fruits is your favourite: apple, orange, banana, pear or pineapple?"**

   This block graph shows their answers:

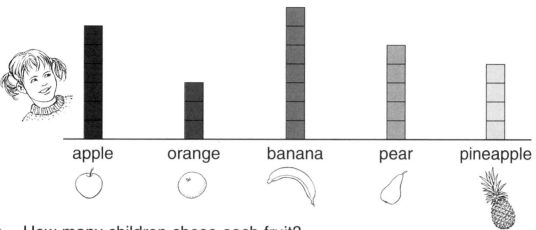

   a. How many children chose each fruit?
   b. Which fruit was most popular?
   c. Which fruit was least popular?
   d. How many more children chose apples than chose oranges?

2. **A group of adults were asked, "Which of these sports is your favourite: football, basketball, tennis, hurling or golf?"**

   This block graph shows their answers:

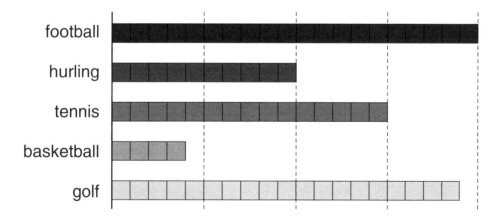

   a. How many people chose each sport?
   b. How many people altogether were asked about their favourite sport?
   c. Which sport was most popular?
   d. Which sport was least popular?
   e. How many more people chose football than chose hurling?

BLOCK GRAPHS

1. **A bicycle factory produces bicycles in 5 different colours: red, black, blue, green and yellow.**

   This block graph shows the number of bicycles of each colour that it produces every week.

   Each block stands for 2 bicycles.

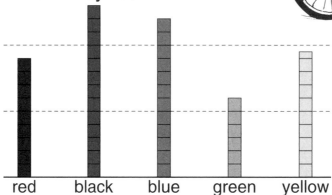

a. What does the half-block at the top of the yellow bar stand for?
b. How many of each colour of bicycle does the factory produce each week?
c. How many bicycles in total does the factory produce each week?
d. Why do you think the factory does not make the same number of bicycles in each colour?
e. If you drew a graph to show the above information, and used one block to represent one bicycle, would your graph use more blocks or fewer blocks than the one shown here?

2. **300 people were asked which of these four films they would most like to see: *The Jungle Book*, *The Lost World*, *Snow White* or *Sleeping Beauty*.**

   This block graph shows their answers. Each block stands for 10 people.

   a. What do the half-blocks at the end of *The Lost World* and *Sleeping Beauty* stand for?
   b. How many people chose:
      i. *The Jungle Book*?
      ii. *The Lost World*?
   c. Which film was most popular?

1. **This bar chart shows the results of a survey of favourite games:**

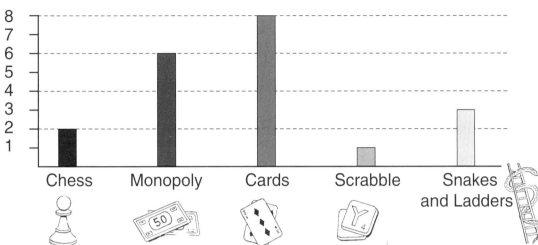

a. How many people chose Monopoly?
b. How many people took part in the survey?
c. Which game was the most popular choice?
d. Which game was the least popular choice?
e. How many more people chose Monopoly
   than chose Snakes and Ladders?
f. Which game would you have chosen?

P 2. **These are the results of a survey of favourite days of the week:**
   Monday 1   Tuesday 5   Wednesday 4   Thursday 8   Friday 9

a. Draw a bar chart to show this information.
   Use a different colour for each bar. Make
   sure all your bars are the same width.
b. Write three questions based on the graph.

PUZZLE POWER

A tree was planted in a forest.
It doubled in height every year.
The tree is now ten years old and
24 metres tall.
When was the tree 12 metres tall?

P 1. **This bar chart shows the favourite colours of a group of people.**
   a. What errors were made in drawing the bar chart?
   b. Draw the chart correctly.

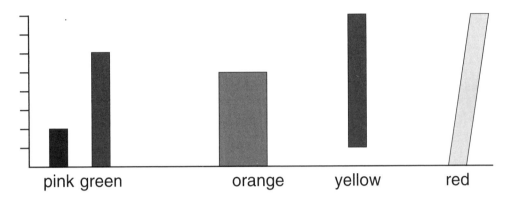

pink green   orange   yellow   red

P 2. **A group of people were asked where in Ireland they would like to go on holiday.**
   Show the results of the survey on a bar chart.

Dingle	6	Courtown	7
Kinsale	5	Connemara	9
Lahinch	4	Bundoran	4

3. **This graph shows a group of people's foreign holiday destinations.**

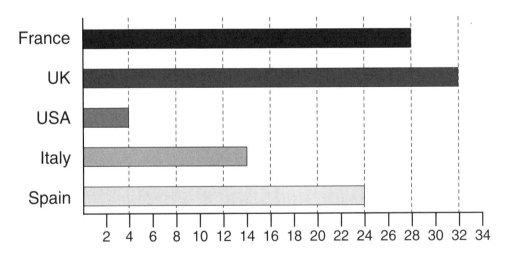

   a. How many people were surveyed altogether?
   b. How many of these went to the USA?
   c. Which foreign country was most popular?
      Give two reasons why you think this is so.
   d. How many people went to either Spain or France?

If you carry out a survey and keep a record of people's answers, this information is called **data**. If lots of people are surveyed and you wish to draw a graph, a page might not be big enough to show all the data unless you use a **scale**. This means counting in twos or fives or tens. In this graph, we counted in fives.

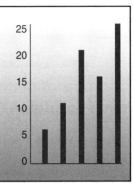

P 1. **Show the results of this survey on a bar chart. Count in twos.**

A group of people were asked which of six names they would choose for a pet dog.

Their answers were:

Sparky 14   Tiger 12   Prince 18   Fred 3   Angel 6   Caesar 10

2. **A group of children were asked which of 5 books they enjoyed most. The 5 books were: *Mike Rofone*, *The Yuckee Prince*, *The Taoiseach's Coat*, *Stanley* and *Return to Troy*.**

Their answers were:

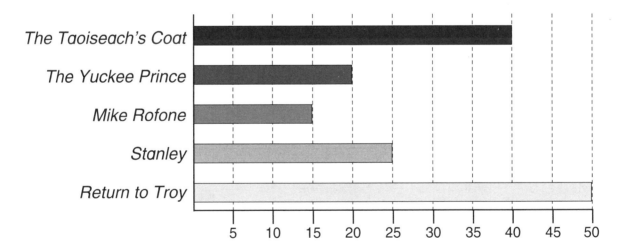

a. Which book was most popular with this group of children?
b. How many children chose *Stanley*?
c. How many children in total were surveyed?
d. Choose 5 popular books and carry out a similar survey in your class.

Sometimes it is better to simply draw a line on a graph instead of a bar. The graph below is a **vertical** bar-line graph.

1. **A group of people were asked which of these flowers they liked best: lilac, carnation, iris, snowdrop or tulip.**

These were their answers. Notice the scale.

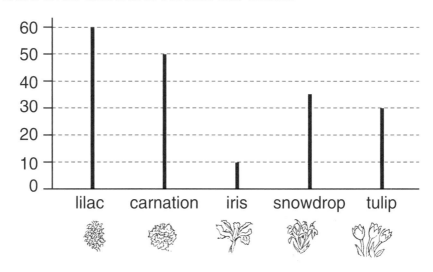

a. How many people chose snowdrops?
b. How many people took part in the survey altogether?
c. How many more people chose a carnation than chose a tulip?
d. Which flower was most popular? Which was least popular?
e. In what way is a vertical bar-line chart different from a horizontal bar-line chart?
f. Which flower would you have chosen?

P 2. **A group of people were asked in which month they usually went on holiday.**

These were their answers:

| April | 5 | June | 25 | August | 50 |
| May | 15 | July | 45 | September | 10 |

Draw a bar-line graph to show these data.
What scale will you use?
a. Why do you think nobody said November, December or January?
b. Why do you think July and August were the most popular months?
c. How many people were surveyed in total?

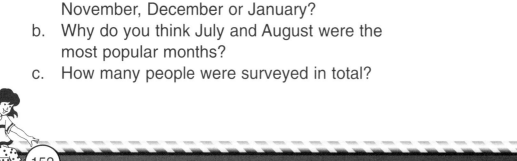

P 1. **One month, a restaurant kept a record of the desserts that people ordered.**

This is a copy of the record:

apple pie	20	ice cream	5	cheese cake	40
trifle	70	pavlova	90	chocolate cake	65

Show the information using a vertical bar-line graph.
What scale will you use?

a. How many people had dessert that month in the restaurant?
b. Why do you think the restaurant carried out this survey?
c. Look at the number of people who chose ice cream in the above survey. What season do you think it was?

2. **A music shop kept a record of the different types of CD it sold one month. Look at the horizontal bar-line graph and answer the questions that follow.**

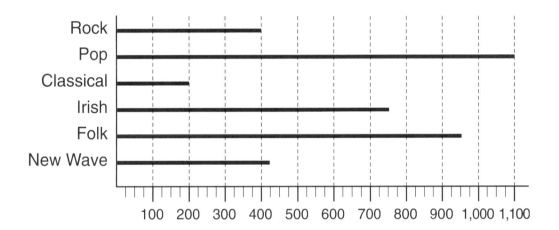

a. How many people bought a pop CD?
b. The number of people who bought an Irish CD is halfway between 700 and 800. How many bought an Irish CD?
c. The number of people who bought a folk CD is halfway between 900 and 1,000. How many bought a folk CD?
d. The number of people who bought a 'New Wave' CD is a quarter of the way between 400 and 500. How many is that?
e. Which type of CD was the most popular?
f. How many more Irish CDs were sold than classical CDs?
g. The owner of the shop wanted to sell 4,000 CDs. How many short of her target was she?

153

1. a. Look at the pie chart.
   i.   What fraction is black?
   ii. What fraction is coloured?
   iii. What fraction is white?

   b. There were 24 children in a class and one day the teacher decided to give each of them a choice of art activity: painting, drawing or colouring.

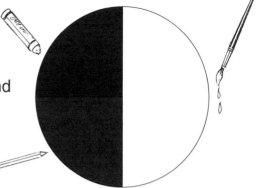

   i. Those that chose painting are represented by the white part of the pie chart. How many chose painting?
   ii. Those that chose drawing are represented by the coloured part of the pie chart. How many chose drawing?
   iii. Those that chose colouring are represented by the black part of the chart. How many chose colouring?

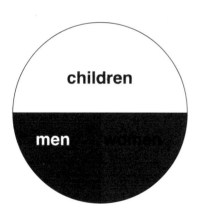

2. **This pie chart represents the one hundred people who went to a circus in a town.**
   Looking at the chart, can you tell how many of these were:
   a. children?
   b. men?
   c. women?

3. a. Is this pie chart divided into equal sections?
   b. What fraction of the whole chart is each section?
   c. The whole chart represents the 72 animals that a farmer had on his farm. How many of each animal did he have?

1.
a. 7 + 6 = ☐
b. 8 + 9 = ☐
c. 12 + 12 = ☐
d. 15 + 16 = ☐
e. 40 + 22 = ☐
f. 20 + 45 = ☐
g. 25 + 16 = ☐
h. 56 + 14 = ☐
i. 44 + 46 = ☐
j. 56 + 36 = ☐
k. 23 + 77 = ☐

2.
a. 9 + ☐ = 10
b. 5 + ☐ = 12
c. 3 + ☐ = 11
d. 11 + ☐ = 22
e. 13 + ☐ = 20
f. 15 + ☐ = 30
g. 20 + ☐ = 36
h. 22 + ☐ = 44
i. 25 + ☐ = 50
j. 31 + ☐ = 50
k. 40 + ☐ = 99

3.
a. 9 − ☐ = 7
b. 8 − ☐ = 8
c. 10 − ☐ = 7
d. 12 − ☐ = 4
e. 15 − ☐ = 9
f. 20 − ☐ = 11
g. 30 − ☐ = 15
h. 50 − ☐ = 41
i. 28 − ☐ = 19
j. 31 − ☐ = 11
k. 35 − ☐ = 0

4. **Match each word sentence with the correct number sentence and work out the answers.**

a. Farmer Murphy has 21 sheep and 14 cows. How many animals has he altogether?

21 − 14 = ☐

b. Farmer Kelly has 21 sheep. He sold 14 of them. How many has he left?

14 + ☐ = 21

c. Farmer Nolan has 14 cows. She would like to have 21 cows. How many more does she need?

21 + 14 = ☐

5. **Put the correct sign (+ or −) between the numbers to make each number sentence true.**

a.
9 ☐ 2 = 11
6 ☐ 3 = 9
7 ☐ 7 = 0
13 ☐ 0 = 13
20 ☐ 12 = 8

b.
13 ☐ 6 = 7
25 ☐ 15 = 10
32 ☐ 12 = 44
48 ☐ 13 = 35
51 ☐ 17 = 68

c.
(5 ☐ 5) ☐ 5 = 15
(6 ☐ 2) ☐ 4 = 4
(10 ☐ 3) ☐ 7 = 6
(11 ☐ 7) ☐ 1 = 3
(12 ☐ 10) ☐ 4 = 6

1. **Match each word sentence with the correct number sentence and work out the answers:**

a. Maria had 72c. She spent 45c. How much money has she left?	45c + ☐ c = 72c
b. Tony had 45c. He wants to buy a comic that costs 72c. How much more does he need?	72c + 45c = ☐ c
c. Orla had 72c in her pocket. She took 45c out of her savings box. How much has she now?	72c − 45c = ☐ c

2. **Write down a correct number sentence for each word sentence. Work out the answers.**

a. Mrs Mulligan had €25 in her purse. She won €50 in a raffle. How much has she now?

b. A fisherman caught 26 fish altogether. Of these, 7 were too small to sell so he threw them back into the water. How many fish had he left to sell?

c. Every time Mr Sweeney shops in Alfie's Supermarket he earns points that he can exchange for gifts. He already has 150 points and he wants a toaster which requires 210 points. How many more points does he need?

d. There are 116 litres of oil in a school's oil tank. How many litres would the delivery person need to put into the tank to fill it if the tank can hold 1,000 litres?

e. An athlete weighed 83·24kg. After 6 weeks of training she lost 6·22kg. What is her present weight?

f. A golfer took 75 shots going around the course on Saturday and she took 73 shots on Sunday. How many shots did she take altogether over the 2 days?

3. **Look at each of these number sentences:**

i. Write an interesting word sentence or problem that would suit each number sentence below.

ii. Answer each question.

a. 45 + 35 = ☐   b. 99 − 88 = ☐

c. 100 − ☐ = 62   d. 125 − 35 = ☐

e. 88 − 40 = ☐   f. 45·11 + 46·33 = ☐

1. What number goes in each box?

a.
```
   4 4
 + 2 □
 ─────
   6 6
```

b.
```
   2 0
 + 4 □
 ─────
   6 7
```

c.
```
   7 1
 + 2 □
 ─────
   9 4
```

d.
```
   7 1
 + □ 5
 ─────
   8 6
```

e.
```
   8 3
 - □ 5
 ─────
   4 8
```

f.
```
   4 4
 - 2 □
 ─────
   2 1
```

g.
```
   5 0
 - 3 □
 ─────
   1 8
```

h.
```
   6 2
 - 5 □
 ─────
   1 1
```

2.
a.   7 x 6 =   □
b.   8 x 9 =   □
c.   7 x 12 = □
d.   5 x 6 =   □
e.   4 x 2 =   □
f.   20 x 4 = □
g.   25 x 4 = □
h.   2 x 14 = □
i.   18 ÷ 3 = □
j.   28 ÷ 7 = □
k.   36 ÷ 9 = □
l.   77 ÷ 7 = □
m.   35 ÷ 7 = □
n.   42 ÷ 6 = □

3.
a.   9 x □ = 18
b.   5 x □ = 35
c.   3 x □ = 15
d.   11 x □ = 66
e.   3 x □ = 36
f.   5 x □ = 45
g.   8 x □ = 72
h.   9 x □ = 63
i.   7 x □ = 0
j.   6 x □ = 6
k.   11 x □ = 110
l.   12 x □ = 48
m.   20 x □ = 40
n.   30 x □ = 90

4.
a.   56 ÷ □ = 7
b.   64 ÷ □ = 8
c.   63 ÷ □ = 7
d.   20 ÷ □ = 4
e.   81 ÷ □ = 9
f.   33 ÷ □ = 11
g.   30 ÷ □ = 15
h.   24 ÷ □ = 4
i.   54 ÷ □ = 9
j.   99 ÷ □ = 11
k.   12 ÷ □ = 1
l.   49 ÷ □ = 7
m.   90 ÷ □ = 10
n.   34 ÷ □ = 17

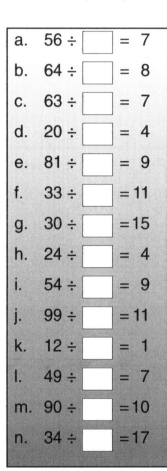

PUZZLE POWER

Gwen ate 80 jellybeans between Monday and Friday. Each day she ate 5 more than she had eaten the day before. How many jellybeans did Gwen eat on Monday?

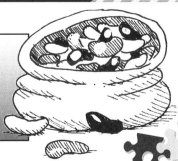

1. **Match each word sentence with the correct number sentence. Work out the answers.**

a. A cinema has 8 rows of seats. In each row there are 24 seats. How many seats are in the cinema altogether?	48 x 12 = ☐
b. A box holds 48 sweets in total. If there are 12 sweets in each layer, how many layers of sweets are in the box?	8 x 24 = ☐
c. If I share €24 equally among 8 people, how much money will each person receive?	48 ÷ 12 = ☐
d. A man earns €48 every day. How much will he earn if he works for 12 days?	24 ÷ 8 = ☐

2. **Put the correct sign (x or ÷) between the numbers.**

a.
6 ☐ 2 = 12
9 ☐ 3 = 27
63 ☐ 7 = 9
11 ☐ 0 = 0
20 ☐ 10 = 2

b.
45 ☐ 9 = 5
56 ☐ 8 = 7
9 ☐ 6 = 54
44 ☐ 11 = 4
12 ☐ 8 = 96

c.
5 ☐ 2 ☐ 2 = 20
6 ☐ 2 ☐ 4 = 48
(24 ☐ 2) ☐ 2 = 6
56 ☐ (16 ☐ 2) = 7
(9 ☐ 6) ☐ 3 = 18

3. **Match each word sentence with the correct number sentence. Work out the answers.**

a. A theatre has 56 seats. There was a full house every night for a week. How many people attended the theatre that week?	5 x 45 = ☐
b. Amy had 45 cards. She divided them into bundles of 5 cards. How many bundles had she?	56 ÷ 7 = ☐
c. A postman has 5 bags of letters to post. There are 45 letters in each bag. How many letters has he to post altogether?	45 ÷ 5 = ☐
d. Paula has 56 jellybeans. How many days will the jellybeans last if she eats 7 every day?	56 x 7 = ☐

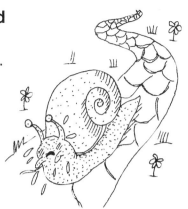

1. **Write down a number sentence for each of these word sentences and work out the answers.**

   a. A snail is crawling along a path that is 21 metres long. How long will it take the snail to reach the end of the path if he crawls 3 metres every hour?

   b. A race track is 1·75km long. How far will a horse travel if he runs around the track three times?

   c. A roof has 126 slates. If there are 9 equal rows, how many slates are there in each row?

2. **Look at each of these number sentences. Write an interesting word sentence or problem that would suit each number sentence. Answer each question.**

   a. 6 x 7 = ☐   b. 63 ÷ 7 = ☐   c. 14 x 6 = ☐   d. 235 ÷ 5 ☐

3. **Work out the rule (x or ÷) and complete each chart.**

   a.

	2	4	9	11	12	10
4		16		44		

   b.

	72	63	9	27	99	81
9		7	1			

   c.

	49	70	14	84	28	56
7		10		4		

   d.

	5	11	1	12	9	4
6			6			24

   e.

	12	72	96	24	48	54
6	2					9

   f.

	12	9	7	2	8	11
9		81		18		

4. **What number goes in each box?**

   a.
   ```
      1 2
   x    ☐
   ------
      3 6
   ```

   b.
   ```
      1 1
   x    ☐
   ------
      6 6
   ```

   c.
   ```
      2 0
   x    ☐
   ------
      8 0
   ```

   d.
   ```
      ☐ ☐
   x    4
   ------
    1 0 0
   ```

5. **Put suitable numbers in each box. There are many possible answers.**

   a. ☐ x ☐ = 24   b. ☐ x ☐ = 25   c. ☐ x ☐ = 40

   d. ☐ x ☐ = 60   e. ☐ x ☐ = 36   f. ☐ x ☐ = 18

   g. ☐ x ☐ = 50   h. ☐ x ☐ = 48   i. ☐ x ☐ = 20

1. **List some liquids that we measure in litres and millilitres.**

1. Orange Juice	5.	9.	13.
2. Cough Medicine	6.	10.	14.
3.	7.	11.	15.
4.	8.	12.	16.

 2. **Colour these containers with the correct amounts of liquid.**

a. **600ml**

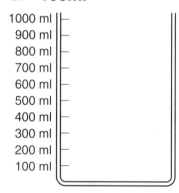

b. **200ml**

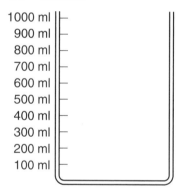

c. **900ml**

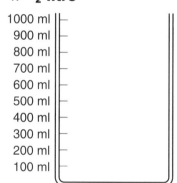

d. **100ml**

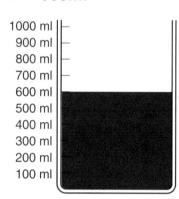

e. **800ml**

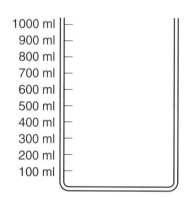

f. **½ litre**

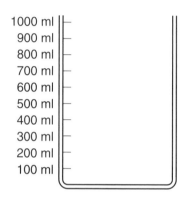

g. **300ml**

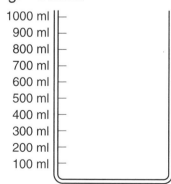

h. **700ml**

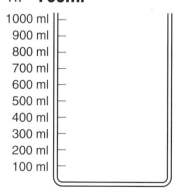

There are
1,000 millilitres
in a litre.
Milk is often sold
in 1 litre cartons.

1. Put each of these items into the correct column according to how much you think it holds when it is full: teacup, bucket, jam jar, yoghurt carton, drinking glass, basin, egg cup, thimble, rubbish bin, kettle.

Less than I litre	About I litre	More than I litre

2. Collect 6 containers. Estimate how many millilitres each container holds when it is full. Then measure the actual capacity. Fill in the chart.

	My Estimate	Capacity	Difference
Mug	300ml	250ml	50ml
Teapot	ml	ml	ml
Jam jar	ml	ml	ml
Beaker	ml	ml	ml
Vase	ml	ml	ml
Drinking glass	ml	ml	ml

3. Estimate capacity in litres.
   Keep your answers to the nearest $\frac{1}{4}$ litre.
   Choose $\frac{1}{4}$ l, $\frac{1}{2}$ l, $\frac{3}{4}$ l, 1l, $1\frac{1}{4}$ l, $1\frac{1}{2}$ l, $1\frac{3}{4}$ l and so on.
   Then measure the capacities. Fill in the chart.

	My Estimate	Capacity	Difference
Kettle	l	l	l
Basin	l	l	l
Watering can	l	l	l
Bucket	l	l	l
Vase	l	l	l

1. **Change each of these to show capacity in litres and millilitres.**
   Example: 2,335ml = 2l 335ml.
   a. 4,557ml b. 2,579ml c. 3,198ml d. 9,561ml e. 8,661ml
   f. 4,300ml g. 8,111ml h. 9,000ml i. 6,008ml j. 4,080ml

2. **Change each of these to show capacity in millilitres.**
   Example: 4l 456ml = 4,456ml.
   a. 4l 462ml b. 3l 451ml c. 1l 559ml d. 3l 333ml e. 4l 654ml
   f. 1l 110ml g. 2l 440ml h. 3l 4ml i. 4l j. 67l

3. a.
l	ml
4	665
+ 3	550

   b.
l	ml
2	339
+ 2	140

   c.
l	ml
8	446
+ 6	500

   d.
l	ml
5	56
+ 3	777

   e.
l	ml
7	70
+ 5	888

4. Bill has 1l 345ml of lemonade in one bottle and 1l 745ml of lemonade in another bottle. How much lemonade does Bill have?

5. A car contains 8l 340ml of petrol. If I add $23\frac{3}{4}$ l, how much will the tank contain?

6. A scientist was working on a new formula. She mixed 1l 867ml of acid with 1l 228ml of water. She then added 333ml of a secret chemical. What amount of the new solution does the test tube contain?

PUZZLE POWER

A farmer is working in one of his fields. He has an empty 5 litre can and an empty 3 litre can. The cans have no markings on them but they measure 5 litres and 3 litres accurately. The problem is the farmer wants to mix some weedkiller with exactly 4 litres of water. (There is a well in the field so there is plenty of water.) How will he measure exactly 4 litres?

1. a.

l	ml
9	445
− 4	351

b.

l	ml
6	347
− 3	556

c.

l	ml
4	440
− 2	67

d.

l	ml
8	449
− 4	556

e.

l	ml
5	8
− 3	855

2. A tank holds 30 litres of water. If 6l 560ml of the water is used, how much water remains in the tank?

3. A car's petrol tank holds 35l 500ml. A motorist filled up the tank with petrol and during the week he used 28l 760ml of it. How much petrol has he left at the end of the week?

4. If I drink 465ml of orange juice from a 2 litre bottle, how much juice will be left in the bottle?

5. a   (3l 236ml + 4l 450ml) − 1l 411ml =

   b. (2l 800ml + 5l 617ml) − 6½l =

6. a. (4l 876ml + 2l 157ml) − 5l 555ml =

   b. (6l 573ml + 2l 135ml) − 56ml =

7. a. 6l 834ml − (2l 230ml + 3l 558ml) =

   b. 7l 300ml − (1l 600ml + 2l 560ml) =

8. a. 10l − (3l 300ml + 4¼ l) =

   b. 8l − (2l 335ml + 7ml) =

9. A pen factory uses 100 litres of ink every day. If 56l 300ml of this is blue ink, 29l 575ml is red ink and the rest is black ink, how much black ink is used?

10. How much milk will be left in a 1 litre carton if I use 180ml of it on my cornflakes and 27ml in my tea?

11. A motorist used 13l 234ml of petrol travelling to Dundalk and 13l 788ml on her way back. If she set out on her journey with 30 litres of petrol in her tank how much has she left?

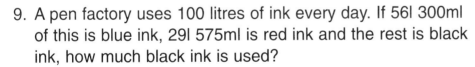

1. **Write as litres using a decimal point. Example: 4l 340ml = 4·34l.**
   a. 5l 670ml b. 2l 340ml c. 1l 130ml d. 4l 480ml e. 7l 600ml
   f. 7l 560ml g. 70l 60ml h. 6l 70ml i. 3,460ml j. 4,400ml
   k. 9l l. 90l m. 90ml n. 60l o. 60ml

2. **Write as litres and millilitres. Example 4·67l = 4l 670ml.**
   a. 5·68l b. 2·34l c. 1·38l d. 8·45l e. 3·57l
   f. 56·34l g. 34·50l h. 3·07l i. 3·7l j. 6·02l

4l 350ml x 6		
Change to a decimal and multiply.	**l** 4·35 $\times\ _2\ _3\ 6$ ——— 26·10	**OR**
	Multiply the litres and millilitres separately.	4l 350ml $\times\ _3\ 6$ ——— 24l 2100ml = 26l 100ml

3. a. 6l 600ml x 6 = ☐   b. 2l 190ml x 6 = ☐

   c. 3l 250ml x 7 = ☐   d. 2l 450ml x 5 = ☐

   e. 3l 40ml x 9 = ☐   f. 6l 20ml x 6 = ☐

4.
   a. **l**
      5·32
      x   2
      ———
   b. **l**
      1·27
      x   5
      ———
   c. **l**
      5·31
      x   7
      ———
   d. **l**
      6·33
      x   5
      ———
   e. **l**
      7·24
      x   9
      ———
   f. **l**
      4·56
      x   8
      ———

5. a. 5l 140ml x 4 = ☐   b. 2l 270ml x 9 = ☐

   c. 9l 350ml x 7 = ☐   d. 7l 160ml x 5 = ☐

   e. 1l 30ml x 8 = ☐   f. 4l 40ml x 6 = ☐

6. A can holds 4l 460ml. How much will 5 such cans hold?

7. Brian drinks 2l 110ml of water every day. How much water will he drink in a week?

8. A painter uses $6\frac{3}{4}$ litres of paint every day. How much paint will he use in 8 days? If paint costs €2·00 per litre how much will the paint cost in total?

9. A bottle of lemonade holds $1\frac{1}{2}$ litres. How much lemonade did a shopkeeper sell if he sold 24 bottles?

1. a. $5 \cdot 76l \div 2 =$ ☐   b. $5 \cdot 43l \div 3$ ☐   c. $6 \cdot 85l \div 5 =$ ☐

2. a. 5l 950ml ÷ 5 = ☐   b. 3l 980ml ÷ 2 = ☐   c. 1l 480ml ÷ 4 = ☐

3. a. 5l 670ml ÷ 9 = ☐   b. 6l 20ml ÷ 7 = ☐   c. 4l 560ml ÷ 8 = ☐

4. A carton of orange juice containing 1l 650ml is shared equally among five people. How much orange juice does each person receive?

5. How many times can I fill a 9 litre container from a tank that holds 200 litres?

6. A central heating system uses 9l 560ml of oil over a period of 2 days. If it uses an equal amount on both days, how much does it use in one day?

7. An aircraft uses 98l 670ml of kerosene during 3 flights. If it uses the same amount on each flight how many litres and millilitres does it use per flight?

8. If you mix 2l 240ml of lemonade with 3l 610ml of fruit juice and share the mixture equally among 9 people. How much will each person receive?

PUZZLE POWER

Match up the questions with the answers and write in the correct letter above the answer.
What do sea monsters eat?

P   1l 230ml x 4 = 4·92l   I   3l 690ml x 23 = ☐

D   2l 140ml x 6 = ☐   S   5l 970ml x 16 = ☐

N   9l 250ml x 9 = ☐

F   7l 750ml x 8 = ☐

A   3l 130ml x 26 = ☐

H   2l 710ml x 29 = ☐

62l	84·87l	95·52l	78·59l			81·38l	83·25l	12·84l

			P	
95·52l	78·59l	84·87l	4·92l	95·52l

1. **Match each picture of a 3-D shape with its name:**

sphere   cube   cone   cylinder   pyramid   triangular prism

a.

b.

c.

d.

e.

f.

2. **Look at this list of items. Say what type of shape each one is:**

   a.   shoe box

   b.   football

   c.   brick for building walls

   d.   dice

   e.   globe

   f.   breakfast cereal box

   g.   matchbox

   h.   ice cream cornet

   i.   tent like this

   j.   traffic bollard like this

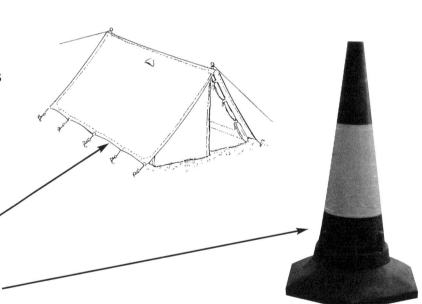

3. **Think of one more everyday example of each of these 3-D shapes:**
   sphere, cube, cone, cuboid, pyramid, prism.

4. Blocks for building walls and houses are always cuboid. Why do you think this is so? Would it be possible to build a wall from pyramids?

1. **Match each set of faces with its 3-D shape:**

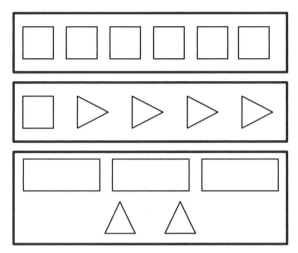

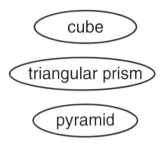

cube

triangular prism

pyramid

PRISMS

A 3-D shape is a **prism** if it is possible to cut through it in such a way that each slice is identical. This cake is a prism because every slice will be the same shape and size.

2. a. **Write its correct name beside each of the 3-D shapes shown below. Choose from the following:**

cube, triangular prism, hexagonal prism, cuboid, pentagonal prism.

b. What shape would a slice of each of these prisms be?

i.

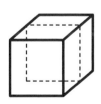

ii.

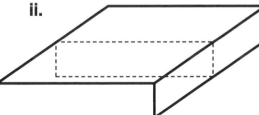

iii.

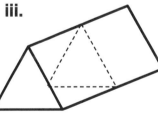

iv.

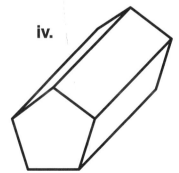

v.

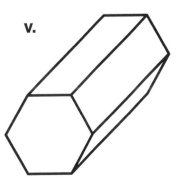

1. Take a glass (or clear plastic) prism and shine light through it. You will make a small rainbow. You could also use a clear plastic pen with the refill removed. Simply hold the prism in sunlight and let it shine onto a sheet of white paper.
    Rainbows in the sky are formed in the same way: little drops of water in the sky act as prisms. Remember never to look directly at the sun – you could damage your eyes.
    Here's a handy way of remembering the seven colours of the rainbow: Richard Of York Gave Battle In Vain.
    Red, Orange, Yellow, Green, Blue, Indigo and Violet.

2. Think of a sentence of your own for remembering the seven colours.

PRISMS

3. a. A square prism has ___ faces.
    b. A triangular prism has ___ faces.
    c. A pentagonal prism has ___ faces.
    d. A hexagonal prism has ___ faces.
    e. What is the smallest number of faces a prism can have?

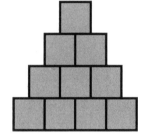

4. Mary was arranging boxes in the pattern you can see in the picture. How many boxes did she use if she had 6 boxes in the bottom row?

PYRAMIDS

Orla bought an unusual cake for her sister's birthday. It was unusual because, as she cut it into slices, the slices kept getting smaller. She had bought a cake in the shape of a pyramid.

5. Which slice would you prefer?

There are many types of pyramid: triangular pyramids, square pyramids, pentagonal pyramids, hexagonal pyramids, and lots more. The **shape of the base** names the pyramid.

1. **Write the name of each pyramid.**

a.

b.

c.

d.

_____ _____ _____ _____

2. **Write the number of faces, edges and vertices (corners) each of these pyramids has:**

a. triangular pyramid:

[ ] faces [ ] edges [ ] vertices

b. square pyramid:

[ ] faces [ ] edges [ ] vertices

c. pentagonal pyramid:

[ ] faces [ ] edges [ ] vertices

edge ⟶

face ⟶

vertex
(vertices)

SIMPLY AMAZING!

THE PYRAMIDS OF EGYPT

The pyramids of Egypt are over 4,000 years old. They are **square pyramids**. The Great Pyramid at Giza is almost 150 metres tall (a modern two-storey house is about 10 metres high). It was built as a tomb for the Pharaoh Khufu. It is made of about 2,300,000 blocks of stone, each block weighing 2,500kg on average. It took over 20 years to build. What is most amazing is that all the blocks of stone had to be cut without any modern machinery, and had to be brought to the building site without as much as a wheel to help. The wheel had not yet been invented!

P 1. **Make your own 3-D shapes.**
   Cut out each shape and fold along the dotted lines.
   Use sticky tape to stick the faces together.

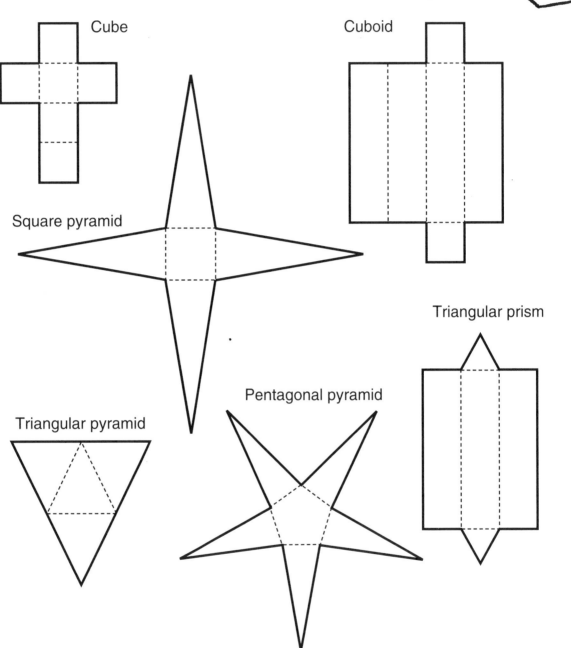

Cube

Cuboid

Square pyramid

Triangular prism

Triangular pyramid

Pentagonal pyramid

2. **Make a cube from:**
   a. 8 Multilink Cubes   b. 27 Multilink Cubes   c. 64 Multilink Cubes

3. **Make a cuboid from:**
   a. 2 Multilink Cubes   b. 10 Multilink Cubes   c. 18 Multilink Cubes

1. Using the 3-D shapes that you have made, count the number of faces, vertices and edges that each one has. Fill in the chart below.

Shape	Faces	Vertices	Edges
Cube			
Cuboid			
Square pyramid			
Triangular pyramid			
Triangular prism			
Pentagonal pyramid			

Hi! My name is Euler. I am a mathematician who lived in the 18th century. If all my work were printed it would fill 75 large books. My most famous discovery was that if you add the number of faces to the number of vertices and then take away the number of edges in any 3-D shape, you will always get the answer 2. This is known as Euler's law.

Example: Let's see if my rule works with the hexagonal prism (remember that pencils are often hexagonal prisms). A hexagonal prism has 8 faces, 12 vertices and 18 edges. So $(8 + 12) - 18 = 2$.

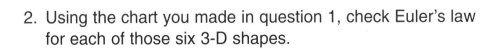

2. Using the chart you made in question 1, check Euler's law for each of those six 3-D shapes.

Let's Look Back (6)

1.
a. 5 x 6 = ☐
b. 11 x 8 = ☐
c. 6 x 5 = ☐
d. 7 x 3 = ☐
e. 9 x 8 = ☐
f. 7 x 9 = ☐
g. 5 x 5 = ☐
h. 3 x 3 = ☐
i. 12 x 5 = ☐
j. 8 x 8 = ☐

2.
a. 7 x 8 = ☐
b. 8 x 12 = ☐
c. 12 x 6 = ☐
d. 6 x 8 = ☐
e. 7 x 1 = ☐
f. 4 x 7 = ☐
g. 3 x 0 = ☐
h. 5 x 4 = ☐
i. 7 x 6 = ☐
j. 4 x 11 = ☐

3.
a. 56 ÷ 8 = ☐
b. 72 ÷ 9 = ☐
c. 32 ÷ 4 = ☐
d. 24 ÷ 2 = ☐
e. 48 ÷ 8 = ☐
f. 56 ÷ 7 = ☐
g. 54 ÷ 6 = ☐
h. 35 ÷ 5 = ☐
i. 63 ÷ 9 = ☐
j. 36 ÷ 3 = ☐

4. Double each of these numbers:
   a. 4   b. 5   c. 11   d. 15   e. 21   f. 25   g. 33   h. 41   i. 52   j. 26

5. Find half of each of these numbers:
   a. 10   b. 12   c. 18   d. 22   e. 30   f. 40   g. 100   h. 42   i. 84   j. 38

6. How many minutes are there in:
   a.   2 hours?   b.   3 hours?   c.   an hour and a quarter?

7. Name a 2-D shape with:
   a.   3 sides   b.   4 sides   c.   5 sides   d.   6 sides

8. Name a 3-D shape with:
   a.   6 faces   b.   5 faces   c.   4 faces   d.   7 faces

9. A television programme started at 7:05 p.m. and finished at 8:15 p.m. How long did the programme last?

10. Write each of these as a fraction:
   a. 0·9   b. 0·7   c. 0·3   d. 0·13   e. 0·29   f. 0·51
   g. 0·79   h. 0·33   i. 0·07   j. 0·09   k. 0·01

11. If you had 3 yellow cubes, 2 red cubes and 1 blue cube in a bag, and you picked one out without looking, which colour is:
   a.   most likely to come out?
   b.   least likely to come out?

12. True or false?
   The cover of this maths book has symmetry.

172

1.
a.
```
   3,446
   2,481
+  1,491
```
b.
```
   2,485
   1,336
+  3,660
```
c.
```
    229
   1,347
+  5,641
```
d.
```
    433
   1,237
+  2,456
```
e.
```
   6,851
     534
+  5,345
```

2.
a.
```
   9,443
-  2,643
```
b.
```
   3,766
-  1,436
```
c.
```
   6,404
-  4,235
```
d.
```
   8,091
-  2,558
```
e.
```
   6,005
-  3,358
```

3.
a.
```
     83
x    60
```
b.
```
     89
x    70
```
c.
```
     46
x    80
```
d.
```
     29
x    90
```
e.
```
    269
x    30
```

4.
a.
```
     65
x    23
```
b.
```
     44
x    25
```
c.
```
     82
x    23
```
d.
```
    167
x    31
```
e.
```
    328
x    23
```

5. a. $716 \div 4 =$ ☐   b. $835 \div 5 =$ ☐   c. $882 \div 9 =$ ☐

   d. $245 \div 7 =$ ☐   e. $616 \div 8 =$ ☐   f. $456 \div 6 =$ ☐

6. Anne and Sue were playing golf. The first hole was 369 metres away from the tee-off position. Anne hit her ball 157 metres and Sue hit her ball 163 metres. How far away from the hole was each golf ball?

7. A pop singer performed in a concert. She came on stage at 8:55 p.m. and sang until 10:40 p.m. For how long was she on stage if she took a ten-minute break?

8. **Let's suppose that today is the 21st of June (the longest day of the year).**
   For how long will the following foods remain fresh?
   (Answer in days.)
   a. Carton of yoghurt with a 'Best Before' date of 24th of June.
   b. Carton of cream with a 'Best Before' date of 28th of June.
   c. Chocolate cake with a 'Best Before' date of the end of the month.
   d. Packet of biscuits with a 'Best Before' date of 4th of July.
   e. Chocolate bar with a 'Best Before' date of 16th of July.

9.
   A jockey weighed 63·4kg and his horse weighed exactly 5 times as much.
   a. What was the weight of the horse and the jockey?
   b. What was the weight of the horse and the jockey and the jockey's pet mouse which weighed 390g?

1. **How much will Billy pay for:**
   a. 7 ice pops @ 14c each?
   b. 6 copies @ 15c each?
   c. 5 pens @ 13c each and a ruler for 21c?
   d. One dozen lollipops @ 8c each?
   e. 11 Fizz Bags @ 9c each?

2. **How much will Billy pay for 2 items if:**
   a. 1 item costs 43c?
   b. 3 items cost 21c?
   c. 4 items cost 44c?
   d. 5 items cost 45c?
   e. 6 items cost 42c?

3. **Which of these do you think is better value for money:**
   a. 3 items for 21c or 2 for 16c?
   b. 3 items for 36c or 2 for 22c?
   c. 4 items for 20c or 5 items for 30c?
   d. 7 items for 56c or 4 items for 36c?
   e. 10 items for 45c or 2 items for 10c?

Oak Lodge Restaurant

Starters
Melon Wedge......€1.25
Prawn Cocktail....€2.35
Mushroom Soup....€1.80

Main Course
Steak & chips......€9.45
Chicken & Chips...€6.95
Fish & chips.......€4.85
Chicken Nuggets...€5.60
Ham Salad........€6.20

Dessert
Trifle............€1.45
Ice-cream.........€1.65

Tea or Coffee............€0.75

4. **Five people went out for a meal. Look at the menu and calculate the cost of each meal:**
   a. Melon wedge, chicken and chips, trifle and coffee.
   b. Mushroom soup, ham salad, ice-cream and tea.
   c. Prawn cocktail, steak and chips and tea.
   d. Fish and chips, trifle and coffee.
   e. Melon wedge, chicken nuggets and coffee.

You will need:
- jar of coffee
- weighing scales
a. Weigh the jar of coffee. This is the **gross weight**.
b. Empty the coffee into another container. Weigh the empty coffee jar. What does it weigh?
c. What must the coffee weigh? This is known as the **net weight**.

1. Claire saw two packets of biscuits in the supermarket. She liked both types of biscuit and both packets were the same price. Packet A was marked 'Net weight – 260g' and Packet B was marked 'Gross weight – 260g'. Which one do you think she bought?

2. A box of breakfast cereal was marked:
Gross weight – 520g   Net Weight – 490 grammes.
What was the weight of the box?

PUZZLE POWER

Make the target number using all three of the given numbers. (Add, subtract, multiply and divide as necessary.) You must use all of the numbers and each number may only be used once. Sometimes there is more than one correct solution.

Example 1: Your numbers are 2, 3 and 4 and your target is 10.
Solution: 2 x 3 = 6   6 + 4 = 10

Example 2: Your numbers are 10, 7 and 7 and your target is 11.
Solution: 7 ÷ 7 = 1   10 + 1 = 11

Remember!
You must use all the numbers and you may only use each number once.

a. Your numbers are 2, 4 and 6 and your target is 0.
b. Your numbers are 3, 5 and 7 and your target is 22.
c. Your numbers are 1, 8 and 9 and your target is 81.
d. Your numbers are 6, 6 and 7 and your target is 48.
e. Your numbers are 8, 8 and 8 and your target is 56.
f. Your numbers are 3, 9 and 10 and your target is 7.
g. Your numbers are 7, 7 and 1 and your target is 1.

1. A swimmer won a race in a time of 54·46 seconds. He was 0·63 seconds faster than the swimmer who finished second. How long did it take the second placed swimmer to swim the distance?

2. If one goal is equal to three points, convert 4 goals and 9 points.

3. If the score in a tennis match was 6-4, 1-6, 6-5, 4-6, 2-6, how many games were played?

4. There are five basketball teams in a group. Each team has to play each other team. How many games will each team play?

5. An archer shoots 36 arrows in a round. Calculate her score for the round if she scored 18 tens, 7 nines, 6 eights, 4 sevens and a miss.

Snooker	
Black	7
Pink	6
Blue	5
Brown	4
Green	3
Yellow	2
Red	1

6. Calculate a snooker player's break if she scored 7 reds, 2 blacks, 3 pinks, 1 brown and 1 yellow.

7. If a runner completes each lap of the track in 52 seconds, how long will it take him to cover a total of 7 laps if he runs the last lap in 49 seconds?

8. How many sports make up a pentathlon?
   (Hint: How many sides has a pentagon?)

9. On a par-4 golf course, a good golfer is expected to take only 4 shots at each hole. How many shots would a good golfer expect to take during a round of 18 holes?

10. A scuba diver wishes to swim to a depth of 38 metres. If she has reached a depth of 20·1 metres, how much deeper has she to swim?

11. A game of hurling lasts 70 minutes. In how many minutes will the referee end the game if 61 minutes have already been played and he allows 2 minutes of injury time?

12. How many runs are there in a century in cricket?

13. A javelin thrower threw her javelin 61·4 metres on her first throw and 62·1 metres in her second. How much further was her second throw than her first?

14. If 9 horses took part in a race, how many legs took part?
    (Don't forget the jockeys' legs!)

15. A crowd of 5,700 attended a recent football final. How much did the organisers collect if they gave out 2,000 free tickets and charged €2 for each of the others?

16. How many car tyres were used in a motorcar race if 22 cars took part and each car changed all its tyres twice?

17. You are providing lunches for the annual soccer blitz. How many sandwiches will you need to prepare if there are 8 teams of 11 players and 4 referees? You expect to give every player 4 sandwiches.